RAILWAYS OF
OXFORD

RAILWAYS OF
OXFORD

A TRANSPORT HUB THAT LINKS BRITAIN

Laurence Waters

PEN & SWORD
TRANSPORT

AN IMPRINT OF PEN & SWORD BOOKS LTD.
YORKSHIRE – PHILADELPHIA

First published in Great Britain in 2020 by
PEN AND SWORD TRANSPORT
An imprint of Pen & Sword Books Ltd
Yorkshire - Philadelphia

ISBN 978 1 52674 038 0

A CIP catalogue record for this book is available from the British Library.

Typeset in Palatino by Aura Technology and Software Services, India.
Printed and bound in India by Replika Press Pvt. Ltd.

Pen & Sword Books Ltd incorporates the Imprints of Pen & Sword Books Archaeology, Atlas, Aviation, Battleground, Discovery, Family History, History, Maritime, Military, Naval, Politics, Railways, Select, Transport, True Crime, Fiction, Frontline Books, Leo Cooper, Praetorian Press, Seaforth Publishing, Wharncliffe and White Owl.

For a complete list of Pen & Sword titles please contact
PEN & SWORD BOOKS LIMITED
47 Church Street, Barnsley, South Yorkshire, S70 2AS, England
E-mail: enquiries@pen-and-sword.co.uk
Website: www.pen-and-sword.co.uk

Or
PEN AND SWORD BOOKS
1950 Lawrence Rd, Havertown, PA 19083, USA
E-mail: Uspen-and-sword@casematepublishers.com
Website: www.penandswordbooks.com

Contents

ACKNOWLEDGEMENTS

I would like to thank the following for their help in producing this book.

In particular Tony Doyle for allowing me to use many of his excellent colour pictures of the area, and Bill Turner for his expertise in restoring some of the early images.

John D. Edwards for the use of his Oxford pictures.

Peter Heath, Peter Simmons, Malcolm Sturges, Peter Bowell, Michael Berry and Graham Carpenter, David Green and Laurence Johnston.

Judith Curthoys, Christ Church College
    Archivist
Liz Woolley, local historian
Colin Harris, Bodleian Library
Helen Drury, Oxford History Centre
Oxford Archaeology
The Bodleian Library Map Room Staff
The Great Western Trust
BMW Mini, Plant Oxford

Ex-Oxford railwaymen: David Benyon, Terry Poole, Alan Wills, Alan Trego, Gordon Goble, John Green, Ted Smith and Peter Allen.

Current Oxford Station staff: Kevin Knight, Station Manager; Warren Bartlett, Deputy Station Manager.

Photography as we know it was not available during the early years of the railway in Oxford, and this means that very few images exist of the area prior to the 1880s. Information on the railway prior to this date can really only be obtained from drawings, maps, plans and reports from the period. To this end early editions of *Jackson's Oxford Journal* and the *Oxford Times* have proved to be invaluable in the description of the early railway scene in Oxford. Images by M. Hale, Mark Yarwood and C.G. Stuart courtesy of Great Western Trust.

All images are from the author's collection unless otherwise acknowledged. Every effort has been made to correctly attribute photographic credits. Should any error have occurred this is entirely unintentional.

Research Sources

Signalling Record Society register of signal boxes.
Peto's Great Western Locomotive registers (Held by the Great Western Trust at Didcot)
Track Layout Diagrams R. A. Cooke
Great Western Magazine 1901–1947
The Railway Magazine
London Evening Standard
Trains Illustrated
Jackson's Oxford Journal
Oxford Times
Oxford Mail

Bibliography

Junctions at Banbury, Barrie Trinder, Banbury History Society, 2017.
Cherwell Valley Railway, Peter Allen, Tempus Books, 1999.
History of the Great Western Railway, Volumes 1, 2 and 3, McDermott, Ian Allan Publishing.

Heart of the Great Western, Adrian Vaughan, Silver Link Publishing, 1995.
Oxfordshire Past and Present, Waters/Doyle, Silver Link Publishing, 1992.
Rail Centres Oxford, Laurence Waters, Ian Allan Publishing, 1986

Laurence Waters
Oxford 2020

INTRODUCTION

I t is difficult today to imagine Oxford without a railway. Prior to its arrival in 1844, goods were transported by canal or by horse and cart, and livestock was still being moved on the hoof. The only way to travel any distance other than by walking or on horseback was by stagecoach. In 1820 there were around 70 stagecoach services arriving and departing from the various coaching inns daily, London being particularly well served with the top service being provided by the 'Rival Coach' which ran from the Angel Inn, High Street, Oxford, to the Bell at Ludgate Hill at a fare of five shillings. Oxford City itself was small and mainly situated around the University which had been founded in the eleventh century. In 1840 the municipal borough population was just 22,000, but arrival of the railway brought speed and comfort for the traveller, as well as expansion to the City in both population and industry. With the opening of the line to Birmingham and beyond in 1852, Oxford became a major through route from the south to the north for both passenger and freight traffic. This, together with the opening of the four local branch lines and the Buckinghamshire Railway branch to Bletchley, made Oxford a major railway hub. The opening of the Great Western/Great Central branch from Culworth Junction to Banbury in August 1900 and the connection to the LMSR (London Midland and Scottish Railway) at Oxford North Junction in 1940 brought even more traffic through the already congested station, with the result that Oxford became an 'operational problem', which in many respects it still is.

My first book on 'Oxford' was published in 1986, some 34 years ago. In the ensuing years the station has been rebuilt twice, and motive power on both passenger and freight traffic has changed considerably, particularly on passenger services. In recent years there has been a major upgrade undertaken on the 'Cotswold' line, as well as the opening of the incredibly successful Chiltern line route from Oxford to Marylebone. Great Western Railway services now comprise a half hourly fast service to and from Paddington interspersed with a half hourly stopping service; added to these are the services to and from the Cotswold line. 'Cross Country' trains now form a major part of the passenger services through Oxford, with a half hourly service to Birmingham and hourly services to Manchester and the north of England. To the south there is a half hourly service to Reading and an hourly service to Southampton and Bournemouth. If into this mix you add in the half hourly Chiltern line services between Oxford and London via Marylebone it is easy to see that Oxford has once again become a very busy station. Today there are more people using the railway at Oxford than at any time since its existence. It is interesting to reflect that along with Exeter, Oxford is now one of the only stations in the country where trains regularly depart daily for London in opposite directions, in this case south to Paddington and north to Marylebone. Although freight traffic has diminished since the 1970s, the regular daily flow of container, car and aggregate traffic ensures that Oxford has a major

railway hub. Future improvements include the construction of a new east–west route between Oxford and Cambridge, and the proposed re-opening of the branch from Kennington Junction to Morris Cowley to passenger traffic. However, although much preliminary work has been completed, electrification of the railway between Didcot and Oxford is still a distant dream, with at the time of writing no date set for a start, let alone completion.

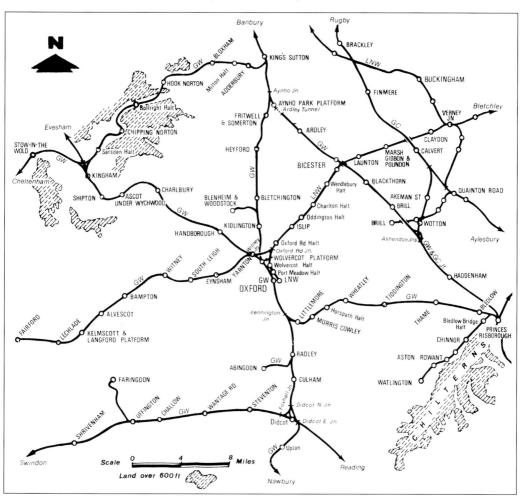

Railway routes around Oxford

Chapter 1

EARLY HISTORY

The Great Western Railway (GWR) deemed that Oxford was important enough to be included in its 1833 prospectus for the construction of its line between London and Bristol, which also included a branch to Oxford. The City is mentioned again in the Directors' half yearly report for 1836 which states 'A branch to Oxford and continuation of it to Worcester are promoted by the leading interests of these two cities, and the best exertions of the Company will be devoted in co-operation with them to accomplish these objects.'

In 1837 a bill for an Oxford Railway was promoted by the Great Western but with the Worcester extension now dropped. The original draft proposal was for a single-track broad gauge branch that would allow for a future double track layout. It would leave the Great Western main line via a junction at Didcot, and would run northwards entering Oxford via Iffley Village, then running east of the Thames, to terminate in a field adjacent to the present plain in the parish of St Clements. This proposal was unsuccessful due to objections from local businessmen, the inhabitants of Iffley Village, and major land owners such as Christ Church. Unperturbed the Great Western tried again, submitting further bills in 1838 and again in 1840. The 1840 proposal contained an important

alteration of the route into Oxford, with the line now running west of the Thames, but once again objectors overruled the plans.

A further bill was presented in 1842 by the newly formed 'Oxford Railway Company' with, of course, considerable support from the Great Western. This time there were fewer objections and importantly the University was generally in favour of the new Oxford branch, but with the proviso that the Company gave an undertaking on the carriage of junior members; basically that they should not be allowed to travel on the railway. This requirement applied to any member below the status of MA or Bachelor of Civil Law, and in order to police this rule University Proctors were to be given free access to the stations at all times to check on this. Failure by the Company to implement this rule would be subject to a £5 fine for each transgression. This strange request had come about because of reports being made to the authorities regarding the increasing number of 'young gentlemen' using the station at Steventon to travel to 'dens of iniquity' such as London, Henley and the races at Ascot.

The station at Steventon had been opened on 1 June 1840 and being the nearest railhead to Oxford was served by up to eight stagecoaches each way daily; a considerable amount of goods traffic also

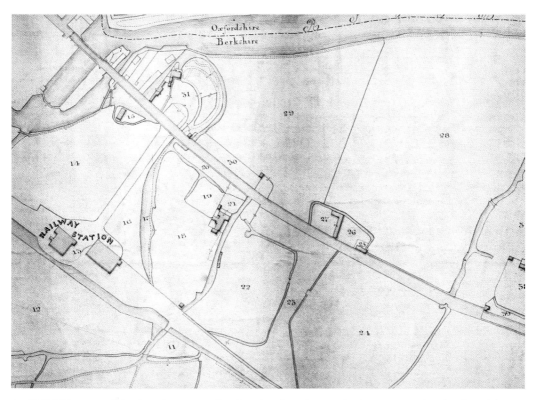

An **1847** Tithe map of the Grandpont area showing site of station. Notice how open and undeveloped the whole area is. (Courtesy Liz Woolley)

traversed the 10 miles between the new station and Oxford City. The stagecoach service was operated by Waddell's coaches and took around 1½ hours at a cost of three shillings. In 1842 it was reported that some 77,567 passengers and 12,620 tons of freight were handled at the station. It appears that Waddell's had the monopoly at Steventon and were the subject of some criticism. In a letter to *The Times* an irate first-class traveller relates suffering a long delay in reaching Oxford, describing the coach that met the train as being: 'already full and occupied by eleven outside and four inside passengers. The coach was moreover top heavy and unsafe from the quantity of luggage and merchandise such as fish, &c, which had been stowed upon it.' With no room he boarded a second coach with two other passengers. He goes on to say, 'In this coach we remained for

exactly one hour and a half' apparently because there was no coachman. On finding a porter he was informed that his coach was not due to depart from Steventon for another hour and a half as it was waiting for the arrival of the Bristol train. On hearing this he remonstrated his anger to the Inspector who then ordered the coach to depart early. He eventually arrived in Oxford at a quarter to ten instead of half past eight. In his letter he clearly blames the Great Western:

> Now I ask is this bearable? Surely the directors should have coaches in sufficient number for the conveyance of their passengers and a van for merchandise; and some distinction should be made between first-class and second-class passengers. I believe I was the only first-class passenger

for Oxford, and yet I was the only one who failed in obtaining a conveyance. The real fact however is that coaching in Oxford is and always has been a monopoly, and that the directors of the Great Western do all in their power to foster this monopoly. No coaches are allowed into the station at Steventon but Waddell's and because this coachmaster chooses to provide insufficient accommodation, the public are to suffer.

Oxford clearly needed a railway, but even in these early days vested interests were being looked after, as one of the more notable objectors to the 1842 Oxford Railway Bill was the Warden of Wadham College. His objection was not on behalf of the College, but as the Chairman of the Oxford Canal Company, which was of course, concerned that trade would be affected with the construction of a railway. However, both the Vice-Chancellor and the University as a whole were generally in favour and on this occasion the objections were overruled, and after three previous abortive attempts Royal

Assent for the new Oxford Railway was granted on 11 April 1843. The bill passed by Parliament was for the construction of a double-track broad gauge line that left the Great Western main line via a junction at Didcot, running northwards for a distance of 9 miles 57 chains to terminate in 'a certain field belonging to Brasenose College on the west of the Abingdon Turnpike Road in the Liberty of Grand Pont and Parish of St Aldate in the City of Oxford and Counties of Oxford and Berkshire or one of them'. On 31 August 1843 the Directors of the newly formed Oxford Railway Company called an extraordinary general meeting at Paddington Station. It was reported that Mr F. Barlow was elected as Chairman of the company, and together with his fellow directors, Robert Gower, Thomas Guppy and Henry Simmonds, was able to report that all of the £120,000 share issue had been taken up. With no local shareholders, it was reported that the entire capital for the Oxford Railway had been put up by the Great Western in the names of 10 of their directors. Mr Thomas Osler was appointed Company Secretary at a

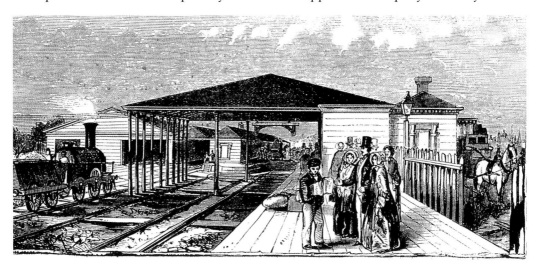

OXFORD STATION.

With no viable photography at this time this Measom drawing is the only image of the old station at Grandpont. It shows the staggered up and down platforms and on the left the large goods shed. (Author's Collection)

salary of £200 per annum. After various resolutions were discussed and passed, the meeting was closed with the final resolution stating:

That the extraordinary and special general meeting of the company to be held this day it be recommended to make a sale of the Oxford Railway Company to the Great Western Railway upon their undertaking to defray all the expenses or charges incident thereto and being subject to the several agreements made by or on behalf of the company.

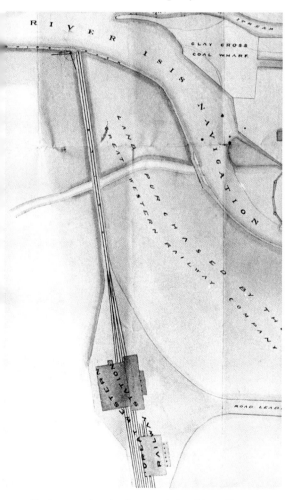

Early map showing layout of the old station at Grandpont. (Author's Collection)

With finances in place and with Brunel as its engineer, work started in October 1843, slightly later than planned due to difficulties in obtaining some of the land; but with the help of a mild winter work progressed at a steady pace, with the majority being completed in late May 1844. The line ran northwards from a junction at Didcot, where a new junction station had been constructed, crossing the River Thames at Appleford and Nuneham via two timber viaducts. On the outskirts of Oxford the line crossed the Turnpike Road to Abingdon and then ran parallel to this road until reaching the terminus which was situated a short distance south of the Thames (Isis) near Folly Bridge. Two intermediate stations were opened at Appleford and at Abingdon Road. This latter station was renamed Culham on 2 June 1856 on the opening of the Abingdon Railway. The station at Culham is interesting as it is built of stone; this is probably due to the influence of the Harcourt family who lived nearby at Nuneham House. For many years a private road connected Nuneham House to the station at Culham. The station at Appleford was situated just to the north of the newly constructed road overbridge which carried the Didcot to Drayton road (now B4016) over the Oxford Railway. One assumes that this station saw little use as it was closed in February 1849.

The line also crossed two main roads, firstly the Dorchester to Abingdon Turnpike Road (now A415) just south of the Abingdon Road station. This was initially crossed on the level until a new brick road overbridge was built in 1845, and again south of Oxford near Kennington where another overbridge would take the Oxford to Abingdon Turnpike Road over the railway. The completion of this section of line was not without drama as the construction of the road bridge was initially delayed by one John Towle, who on hearing that the railway was under construction decided to erect a paper house on part of the proposed site of the bridge. Towle, who was a bit of an eccentric, probably saw this as an opportunity to obtain compensation from the railway. In his inspection report prior to the opening of the line Major-General Charles Pasley noted that one arch of the bridge was insecure and that:

> Mr Brunel explained to me that the haste with which this arch of the bridge was built was caused by the conduct of an individual in possession of part of the ground over which the embankment was carried, who after the site of the bridge had been decided on, erected what he called a 'house' which I saw but should never have guessed the use of, being a small hut of timber framework covered with brown paper, with a fireplace in it, for the purpose of claiming compensation from the Railway Company for having diminished the value of his property; and the work was delayed as the unexpected claim could not be settled until the period of the entire completion of other parts of the railway.

History does not record whether Mr Towle received his compensation but the railway opened on time, initially crossing the road on the level until the new bridge (known locally as Redbridge) was completed a few days later. John Towle became a well-known local councillor and magistrate and was elected Mayor of Oxford in 1856. He continued to live in his paper house which he ironically named 'Pasley House' until his death on 18 February 1885.

On Monday 10 June 1844 and prior to the official opening, a special train from Paddington to Oxford carrying the Directors of the Company, accompanied by 25 ladies, noblemen and other guests that included Brunel, Major-General Pasley and Charles Saunders, the secretary of the Great Western. It was reported that a satisfactory run was made, with Didcot (53 miles from Paddington) being reached in 1hr 8min. The London *Evening Standard* of 15 June 1844 newspaper also reported that:

> From Didcot to Oxford the train travelled slowly to give the Inspector (Major-General Pasley) the opportunity of making the necessary survey; on arriving at Appleford Bridge the centres had not been struck and caused the steps of the carriages which hit against them to be twisted nearly off. The force was such that it is supposed that had the train been on a narrow gauge of line instead of the broad one of the Great Western, it must have inevitably been driven off, and the consequences might have been fatal. The train however arrived at Oxford at half past two.

On arriving at the new terminus, it was reported that 'the fifty-four strong party proceeded to the Angel Inn, High Street, where a splendid luncheon awaited them. After much rejoicing the party returned to Paddington by special train at about 4 o'clock.' Obviously the earlier problem with the bridge had been resolved.

With no effective photography available to record events at this time we have to rely on newspaper reports to paint a picture of the occasion. *Jackson's Oxford Journal* reported that:

> The line was opened for passengers and the conveyance of goods, on Wednesday morning (12 June 1844) and the advantages of comparative speed and safety, which the trunk-line possesses, are partaken by this extension branch. The

GREAT WESTERN RAILWAY.
OPENING TO OXFORD.

On WEDNESDAY, the 12th of JUNE, 1844, the Oxford Railway will be opened for the Conveyance of PASSENGERS, Carriages, Horses, and Goods.

STATIONS AT DIDCOT JUNCTION, ABINGDON ROAD, AND APPLEFORD, WILL ALSO BE OPENED.

This Railway is now Completed to Exeter, Taunton, Bristol, Bath, &c.

EXETER is 45 miles from PLYMOUTH; CIRENCESTER is 15 miles from CHELTENHAM, 12 miles from STROUD, and 17 miles from GLOUCESTER.

Horses and Carriages being at those Stations, which are distinguished by Black Letter Type, ten minutes before the time specified for the departure of a Train, will be conveyed on this Railway. Horses only are conveyed to and from West Drayton.

The stones black marks or stops, under certain times of arrival shew, that the Trains do not proceed beyond the Stations on the same line with them.

POST HORSES are kept in readiness at the principal Stations, and upon sufficient notice being given at Paddington, or at the Bull and Mouth Office, St. Martin's-le-Grand, would be sent to bring Carriages from any part of London to the Station, at a charge of 9s. west of St. Martin's Lane, and 10s. 6d. beyond it, both including Post Boy. Similar notice may be given at Bristol for Carriages to be brought from Clifton or the neighbourhood, to the Bristol station.

LONDON TIME is kept at all the Stations on the Railway, which is 4 minutes earlier than READING time; 5½ minutes before OXFORD time; 7½ minutes before CIRENCESTER time; 8 minutes before CHIPPENHAM time; 11 minutes before BATH and BRISTOL time; and 14 minutes before EXETER time. No Tickets will be issued after a Train is in sight at the intermediate stations.

The Royal Hotel at Slough, and Railway Hotel at Reading, are open.

TIME TABLE.

17 June, 1844.

J. L. COBBIN, PRINTER, ALDERSGATE STREET.

Turn over.

Great Western timetable showing opening of the Oxford Railway, 12 June 1844. (Author's Collection)

Firefly Class 2-2-2 *Argus*, built by Felton, Murray & Jackson of Leeds, in August 1842. Locomotives of the Firefly Class were used to haul the first passenger services to and from Oxford. (Author's Collection)

Oxford station is not quite finished but is in a forward state. There are separate platforms for the arrival and departure of trains.

The *Evening Standard* newspaper also reported that the:

First train departed from Oxford at ten minutes to eight o'clock in the morning and that there were not as many passengers as might have been expected. It arrived safely at Didcot in about 26 minutes. The line was exceedingly smooth, and the riding pleasant and comfortable, being another confirmation of the superiority of the broad gauge over the narrow one used in the North of England.

The line of rail between Oxford and Abingdon Road station, a distance of about 7 miles, commands a view of the countryside, one of the most beautiful that can be imagined. Passing Hinksey it crosses the road to Abingdon, about one and a quarter miles from Oxford, under a brick bridge it passes on a short distance from the Isis, through Kennington, by Sandford to Nuneham, the seat of the Archbishop of York, where it crosses the water and shortly arrives at the Abingdon station, a pretty building of brick and stone, situated about 3 miles from Abingdon. Another mile and we are at Appleford station, a temporary shed. After passing under another brick bridge, then 2 miles of uninteresting country and we are at Didcot.

The report is less than complimentary about Didcot describing it as 'A village of a most – we were going to say – rueful, we suppose it will be better to say rural aspect; frightened out of its propriety by the notoriety it has lately assumed in being

There were two intermediate stations opened on the Oxford Railway, at Appleford and Culham. The first original station at Appleford was situated on the north side of the road overbridge, it closed in 1849. The second station at Appleford stood south of the bridge and was opened on 11 September 1933. It is pictured here in 1957, still with its Pagoda waiting rooms. (Author's Collection)

the place of junction with a branch line to the Great Western.' The report goes on to describe the station as 'the temporary wooden station, erected or being erected, is, we imagine from its scantiness, intended to last only a few days.'

Initially the service comprised nine trains a day in each direction, plus a third-class and luggage train. These early services would almost certainly have been hauled by members of the Firefly Class 2-2-2s. The first departure from Oxford was at 7.50am, with the first arrival at 8.10am; all of these services stopped at Abingdon Road but just three trains each way stopped at Appleford. The average journey time between Oxford and Didcot was 30 minutes. These early broad gauge trains were often formed of just five or six vehicles, carrying perhaps between 100–200 passengers. Return fares from Oxford to Paddington at this time were: first-class 15 shillings; second-class 10 shillings; and third-class 6 shillings (one train a day). In today's money

these fares relate to approximately £59, £38, and £20. The fares were the subject of much local criticism, with the press declaring that they were:

> Much too high and will materially operate against the line, more especially while the public have the opportunity of sitting behind Charles Holmes and his splendid greys all of the way to town, through beautiful country, for 5 shillings. The rail in consequence be no boom to the humble tradesman or mechanic and is not likely to be patronised much, except by those who have ample means or have urgent business to transact.

This was an interesting statement, as in 1839 it was reported that the average journey time for a stagecoach between Oxford and London was around eight hours, which must have been particularly uncomfortable due to the poor quality of the roads at this time.

The second station on the branch opened as Abingdon Road, then with the opening of the Abingdon branch in 1856 it was renamed Culham. The station is seen here in 1958 as Hall Class No. 5983 *Henley Hall* arrives with an up stopping service. The main station building is now a listed structure and still survives in commercial use (see colour section) but the signal box, down station building and the ex broad gauge goods shed have long gone. (J. D. Edwards)

It is hard to imagine today just what an impact the arrival of a railway had on the various towns and villages in this country, and the City of Oxford proved to be no exception. The opening of the Oxford Railway was greeted by large crowds, with special attractions such as a gala day at Hinksey field and at South Hinksey where marquees, tents, stalls and exhibitions were set up for the opening, with parties and celebrations going on late into the evening. At this time the whole area south of the City consisted mainly of open fields. It was suggested by the local press that for those wishing to view the railway that a good view of the arrival and departure of trains could be seen from the nearby Folly Bridge, and that the 'carriages can be plainly seen sweeping along with great rapidity from the Henley Road between St Clement's and Rose Hill.'

The *Journal* also described the new line thus: 'The line from Oxford to Didcot is a remarkably easy one, and embraces scenery that is both beautiful and interesting, and will not fail to delight all who travel on it more especially to those who are strangers to Oxford and its neighbourhood.' It adds: 'The scenery to Didcot is beautiful and a fine view of the Archbishop of York's residence at Nuneham is obtained by the passengers.' It goes on to report that 'the City has been crowded since Wednesday with parties

GREAT WESTERN.

Dis. Miles	UP TRAINS. STATIONS.	WEEK DAYS. 1st & 2nd Class	1st & 2nd Class.	1st & 2nd Class.	1 2 & 3 Class.	1 2 & 3 Cla. *	1st & 2nd Class.	1 2 & 3 Class	1st & 2nd Class	SUNDAYS. 1 2 & 3 Class.	1 2 & 3 Class.	1st & 2nd Class
	Starting from	A. M.	A. M.	A. M.	A. M.	P. M.	P. M.	P. M	P. M	A. M.	P. M.	P. M.
	BIRMINGHAM ..	6 40	..	7 40	11 15	12 0	2 30	2 45	5 15	10 30	3 15	6 45
4	Acock's Green......	..	..	7 50	..	..	..	..	..	10 40	3 25	6 55
6¾	Solihull	..	..	7 55	11 29	..	..	3 0	5 29	10 41	3 30	7 0
10¼	Knowle	..	..	8 5	11 38	..	..	3 8	5 38	10 54	3 40	7 10
17	Hatton...........	..	..	8 20	..	..	..	3 23	..	11 10	3 56	7 26
21	Warwick..........	7 15	..	8 30	11 59	12 38	3 8	3 33	5 58	11 20	4 6	7 36
23¼	Leamington........	7 22	8 0	9 0	12 7	12 45	3 15	3 41	6 6	11 30	4 15	7 45
29¼	Harbury	..	8 12	9 15	12 21	..	..	3 55	6 20	11 45	4 30	8 0
33¼	Fenny Compton....	..	8 23	9 27	12 30	..	..	4 7	6 31	11 55	4 42	8 12
39¼	Cropredy..........	..	8 33	9 40	..	..	..	4 19	..	12 5	4 55	8 25
42¾	BANBURY	7 57	8 40	9 50	12 50	1 20	3 55	4 30	6 48	12 15	5 5	8 35
48¾	Aynho	..	8 52	10 3	1 5	..	..	4 45	7 2	12 29	5 18	8 48
53¾	Heyford	..	9 2	10 13	1 15	..	..	4 57	7 14	12 40	5 30	9 0
57¾	Woodstock Road ..	..	9 10	10 22	1 25	..	..	5 7	7 24	12 50	5 40	9 10
65¾	Oxford } Arrival ..	8 40	9 25	10 37	1 40	2 0	4 35	5 25	7 40	1 20	5 55	9 25
	Oxford } Departure	8 42	9 30	10 45	1 45	2 5	4 40	5 30	7 45	1 30	6 0	..
72¾	Abingdon Road	..	9 45	11 0	2 0	..	..	5 46	8 0	1 45	6 15	..
75¾	Didcot	9 0	9 55	11 8	2 10	2 25	5 2	5 55	8 10	1 55	6 25	..
128¾	PADDINGTON ..	10 45	11 25	1 10	7 20	4 5	6 40	8 15	10 15	5 0	8 30	..

* Third Class from Birmingham to Oxford, inclusive to London.

The train leaving Birmingham at 2.45 p.m. calls at Somerton at 4.50.

Dis. Miles	DOWN TR STATIONS.	WEEK DAYS. 1 2 & 3 Class.	1 2 & 3 Class	EXP. 1st & 2nd†	1st & 2nd Class.	1st & 2nd Class	1 2 & 3 Cl. ‡	1st & 2nd Class.	EXP 1st & 2nd	1st & 2nd Class.	SUNDAYS. 1st & 2nd Class.	1 2 & 3 Class.	1st & 2nd Class
	Starting from	A. M.	A. M	A. M.	A. M.	P. M	P. M.	P. M.	P. M.	P. M.	A. M.	A. M.	P. M.
	PADDINGTON	6 0	*6 50	9 45	11 0	11 45	2 0	2 45	4 50	6 15	..	9 0	2 0
53	Didcot	7 50	11 0	Passengers leaving Paddington by this train arrive at Didcot in time for the train leaving that station for Birmingham at 11.0.	12 30	1 40	3 40	4 42	6 15	7 45	..	11 5	4 3
56	Abingdon Rd	8 5	11 10		..	1 50	3 50	5 10	6 25	..	..	11 12	4 12
63	Oxford	8 20	11 25		12 55	2 10	4 10	5 25	6 40	8 3	9 0	11 20	4 28
71	Woodstock Rd	8 48	11 46		..	2 32	4 31	5 46	7 0	..	9 15	11 45	4 45
75	Heyford	8 58	11 56		..	2 42	4 40	5 56	7 10	..	9 25	..	4 55
80	Aynho	9 11	12 9		..	2 55	4 52	6 9	7 23	..	9 37	..	5 7
86	BANBURY..	9 25	12 23		1 40	3 10	5 5	6 23	7 40	8 48	9 50	12 7	5 20
89½	Cropredy	9 35	12 33		..	3 18	..	6 33	7 50	..	10 0	..	5 30
94½	Fenny Comp.	9 47	12 45		..	3 30	..	6 46	8 1	..	10 13	..	5 43
99½	Harbury	9 59	12 58		..	3 42	..	6 58	8 11	..	10 25	..	5 55
105½	Leamington ..	10 12	1 12		2 15	3 52	5 38	7 30	8 25	9 28	10 40	12 40	6 10
107¾	Warwick	10 20	1 20		2 23	4 0	5 45	7 38	..	9 35	10 49	12 48	6 19
111¾	Hatton	10 30	1 30		..	4 10	..	7 48	..	..	10 59	12 56	6 29
118½	Knowle......	10 45	1 45		..	4 25	..	8 4	..	..	11 14	1 14	6 44
122	Solihull......	10 53	1 53		..	4 33	..	8 15	..	..	11 24	1 24	6 54
124¾	Acock's Green	10 58	1 58		..	4 48	..	8 20	..	..	11 29	1 30	6 59
128¾	BIRMINGHAM	11 10	2 10		3 0	5 0	6 20	8 30	..	10 15	11 40	1 45	7 10

* First and Second Class Passengers may leave Paddington at 7.40. † This is Express to Didcot only. ‡ Third Class arrive at Banbury at 6.23.

The 6.0 a.m. from Paddington calls at Somerton at 9.4.

Day Tickets usually at a reduction of one-fourth of the double fare, and available for the same day, will be issued to First and Second Class Passengers. Saturday Tickets will be returnable on the day they are issued, or on the following Sunday or Monday. Sunday Tickets, in like manner, will be returnable on the day they are issued, or on the Monday following. The Express Train from Birmingham at 8.20 a.m., and 7.30 p.m., and from Paddington at 9.45 a.m and 4.50 p.m., do not stop at Banbury, but pass that station about 9.20 a.m.; 8.30. p.m 11.55. a.m. and 7 5. p.m. Parcels may be booked at any of the Company's Stations for conveyance to the different Stations on the Line.

The 1852 Paddington to Oxford and Birmingham timetable. (Author's Collection)

A **view** of Kidlington taken in 1934. Opened as Woodstock Road on 1 June 1855 it was renamed Kidlington on 19 May 1890. On the right is the Woodstock Branch bay and the small goods yard and shed. The sidings were extended during 1923 to serve the Oxfordshire Farmers Bacon Factory Ltd that was opened in November 1923 and which can be seen in the distance. The factory was taken over by C. T. Harris (Calne) Ltd in 1930 and production continued until 1960 when the factory was closed. The station was closed to passengers on 2 November 1964 and to goods a year later. Today all trace of the station has gone and the yard is part of the 'Station Field' industrial estate. (Author's Collection)

from the county, led by the curiosity to see the wonders of locomotion by steam.' Obviously the high fares did not detract the public from using the railway as it was reported that during the first week of operation 'the trains from Didcot have been tolerably well filled.'

The opening of the line resulted in a number of local entrepreneurs becoming ticket agents. One early ticket agent was William Thompson, who operated from No. 59 High Street as a carver, gilder, picture framer and print seller. But probably the most important local railway ticket agent was Joseph Plowman, who at this time was a well known Oxford businessman and inventor. He traded for many years from No. 1 St Aldates, selling cigars and tobacco, and became an agent for the Railway Passenger Assurance Company; he also ran the City Reading Room and Library. Records indicate

that both Plowman and Thompson were involved during the early 1850s in organising some of the first excursion trains from Oxford.

From the outset the Great Western and Brunel in particular saw the opening of a branch to Oxford as the first part of an expansion by the Company northwards to Birmingham, Wolverhampton and beyond. In 1844 the Oxford & Rugby Railway Company had been formed as a subsidiary of the Great Western to construct a 51 mile line from Oxford to connect with the London & North Western Railway at Rugby. The new line would run via Banbury, Fenny Compton and Southam. Royal Assent was obtained on 4 August 1845 and work was started on the first part of the line from Oxford to Banbury during the following year. This first section to Banbury was opened for passenger traffic on Monday

2 September 1850. However, another bill by the Birmingham and Oxford Junction Railway to construct a line from Fenny Compton to Birmingham via Leamington, a distance of 42¾ miles, received Royal Assent on 3 August 1846. This new direct route to Birmingham and Wolverhampton sounded the death knell for the Oxford and Rugby Railway, which having reached Fenny Compton was abandoned in favour of the Oxford and Birmingham route.

The first part of the extension to Banbury was initially constructed as a single-track broad gauge line, but with provision made from the start to eventually double the track. This gradually took place as the line was extended further northwards to Birmingham, and at the same time mixed gauge was introduced over the route. This latter requirement was made on orders from the Board of Trade. Initially services from Oxford to Banbury operated to and from the terminus at Grandpont, running via Millstream junction; this required trains to reverse in and out of the terminus station. The Board of Trade report on the opening of the extension to Banbury provides an interesting description of the route:

> The line begins at Millstream Junction, three quarters of a mile south of the Oxford terminus station, near the Abingdon Road Bridge. One bridge over the River Isis at Oxford consists of three openings, constructed of wrought iron, with the centre opening measuring 62ft and the two end ones 32ft. The other bridges carrying the Railway are principally timber framed and cast iron. There are only three stations: Woodstock, Heyford and Aynho.

Bletchington was opened by the Oxford and Rugby Railway on 2 September 1850 as Woodstock Road. In 1855 it was renamed Kirtlington and on 11 August 1890 as Bletchington. It was closed on 2 November 1964. The goods yard on the left closed on 21 June 1965. The station is pictured here around the turn of the last century. The Stationmaster's house, which still survives as a private dwelling, can just be seen on the right. (Author's Collection)

Heyford was also opened by the Oxford and Rugby Railway on 2 September 1850; the station is seen here in the early 1900s. Six members of the station staff pose for the photographer. Heyford is still open and served by Great Western services between Oxford and Banbury. (Author's Collection)

Woodstock was renamed Woodstock Road in May 1851, Kirtlington in July 1855 and finally Bletchington on 11 August 1890. The local newspaper reported that:

> The railway opened with no public demonstration on the occasion. The first train from Banbury left at half past eight and the first from Oxford soon after ten. There are four trains daily each way and they have been running during the week with much regularity and with as fair an allowance of passengers as could be expected.

However it was not all good news:

> There was a unanimous level of disappointment and dissatisfaction at the first train from Oxford not reaching Banbury before 11.15am, a time that will be too late for the dealers (at Banbury Market and on Fair days) and that the last train from Banbury to Oxford leaving at 4.05pm, an hour that everyone admitted was much too early for those who had business to transact.

Interestingly, the section of the line between Millstream Junction and the new station at Oxford was raised above the Hinksey flood plain using gravel and spoil dug up from a field adjacent to the railway. With the water table being high at this point the excavated area soon filled with ground water, thus forming what is now known as Hinksey Lake. In 1854 the Oxford Corporation purchased the lake for use as a reservoir to supply its new water pumping station which opened in 1856 at the end of what is now Lake Street. The waterworks were closed in 1934, with the adjacent area becoming part of Hinksey Park. The old brick pumping station building still survives, and is currently in use as a community centre.

The rather inconvenient reversal manoeuvre at Millstream junction ceased with the opening of the new through station at Oxford on 1 October 1852. The new station was situated approximately ½ mile northwards and adjacent to the Botley Road. The terminus station at Grandpont was then closed to passenger traffic, although it remained open as a goods station until the removal of the broad gauge locally in December 1872. The opening of the new station coincided with the opening of the Great Western line through to Birmingham. What should have been a celebration nearly turned into a disaster when on Wednesday 29 September a special Directors' train comprising 10 carriages and hauled by one of Gooch's 8ft singles *Lord of the Isles* with both Gooch and Brunel on the footplate collided with a passenger train at Aynho. It seems that the special train started from Paddington shortly after 9am but owing to a number of delays it did not reach Oxford until 10.50am instead of 10.15. At Oxford many local dignitaries boarded the train, which delayed it further. In the meantime the ordinary stopping service from Oxford to Banbury, which should have left Oxford at 9.55am, departed some 23 minutes late and had reached Aynho, where the tickets were being collected on the train. The local newspaper reported that:

> The special from London was seen approaching at a rapid pace. The driver of the Banbury train immediately put his engine in motion to prevent it from being run into, unfortunately the coupling chain between the two passenger carriages and the three luggage trucks snapped asunder. At an instant the engine of the special train ran into the hindmost luggage van forcing that and the two others preceding it along the line until they came in contact with the passenger carriages.

> The severe blow struck by the express engine against the weighty luggage vans threw it off the line and after ploughing up the ground for some dozen yards, breaking off the switches and tearing up the transoms, came into contact with the masonry of the platform, and was finally brought to a standstill. Every effort was made by Mr Brunel and Mr Gooch who were with the engine driver to bring up the train in order to avoid a collision, but owing to the short distance it was impossible to do so. Notwithstanding that all brakes were applied and steam was reversed.

The collision resulted in several of the passengers in the second-class carriage of the Banbury train being cut and bruised, although with the exception of Mr and Mrs Berry of Upper Heyford and Elizabeth East, a servant at the King Arms, Deddington, who were injured on the face and head, the rest proceeded on their journey to Banbury. Brunel, who had travelled to Banbury on the stopping train, returned to Aynho with the engine from the stopping service. *Lord of the Isles* was soon moved to an adjacent siding and with the line having been cleared, the special left for Leamington hauled by this engine, arriving at around 2pm. With such a delay the special party that comprised some 200 ladies and gentlemen proceeded to the Royal Hotel Leamington, where they took dinner. It was reported that speeches were made celebrating the opening of the railway, but I would imagine with some degree of disappointment and embarrassment. The report concludes that 'it is satisfactory to contemplate how little damage has been done, and how miraculously a large number of persons have escaped injury, if not premature death.' The subsequent enquiry concluded that the driver of the special had insufficient knowledge of the line and had mistaken a disused signal that controlled a temporary ballast siding and had been left in the all clear position as the main line signal. He then proceeded to pass the proper main line signal that had been set at danger, with obvious consequences.

Such was the nature of the day that another Gooch single, *Sultan*, which was sent for from Birmingham to render assistance at Aynho was itself derailed *en route* and was apparently 'embedded in the sand for several hours'. It was reported that as a result of the collision at Aynho *Lord of the Isles* had its 'buffers broken off, the gearing irons stripped away and its front wheels knocked from their frames'. The following day it was removed to Swindon for repair.

With its close proximity to the Thames and its tributaries, flooding has always been a problem at Oxford as the Great Western was soon to find out. The autumn of 1852 was particularly wet, which resulted in many areas being flooded. A particularly bad spot was at Kennington, a low lying area to the South of the City. Here the line flooded to such an extent that trains could not pass. A Board of Trade report dated 4 November 1852 stated that:

On the evening in question the trains from London were unusually late. The delay was caused at Oxford in consequence of the floods from the very great quantity of rain which had fallen having rendered a portion of the line impassable for engines, in consequence of which it was necessary to draw the trains through the water by means of horses. The trains from London were stopped at Kennington Crossing between two and three miles south of the (new) Oxford Station and about a quarter of a mile south of the water.

The engine was here shifted to the rear of the carriages, which it pushed to the water's edge; horses were then harnessed to them, and the carriages were drawn by them through the water. At the other side the engine that was to take the train on from Oxford was waiting; this engine was accompanied by a pilotman, who received his instructions from an Inspector of Police, who was situated on the south side of the water. The actual time required to pass a train through the water was about 12 minutes.

Over the ensuing years flooding in this area has proved to be a recurring problem, on occasions delaying or even stopping services. Unbelievably it was not until 2015 that the line was raised and the drainage improved in this area.

It was not just floods that delayed the trains. On Tuesday 18 January 1881 the Oxford area was hit by what was described as 'A Great Snowstorm' which affected all railway services in the county and particularly over the section between Culham and Oxford. The local newspaper reported that south of the City 'the lines were blocked in each direction and that telegraphic communication was also interrupted due to the breaking of the poles wires due to the wind and snow.' The report continues:

The last train which entered the Great Western station on Tuesday was the 3.30 from Paddington, which arrived very late, and then there was a total cessation of traffic on the down line until Wednesday evening, when a portion of the train which left London on the previous afternoon came in at 6.30 with a few passengers, and was followed about an hour later by the other part of it. The train had been snowed up

Similar floods occurred in 1875 and 1894. In 1875 the flooding was so severe that it effected the area adjacent to the station as seen here. The Jackson's Oxford Journal 20 November 1875 reported St Thomas's Osney and all low lying places were flooded to a considerable distance on each side between 9 and 10ft, thus rendering the road impassable. A punt was used at first for the conveyance of passengers by train to the station. The water in the tunnel under the station was several feet in depth, and the wooden flooring was torn from its position and floating to the top. (Oxford History Centre)

at Radley and the passengers who included the Dean of Christ Church, Mrs Liddell, and the two Misses Liddell, appear not to have suffered from their long detention in the snow.

The last up service to leave was the 4.5pm express service to Paddington. This apparently took some time to reach Radley, and came to a stand north of Culham at about 5.30pm. The newspaper report goes on to say:

That the violence of the gale and snow combined, prevented the carriage doors from being opened, and soon the train became completely embedded in the snow. The lights were of course put out by the

snow, and the passengers were left in total darkness. No aid reached them until past eight-o'clock the following morning when the sound of shovels was heard and after some hours work their release was at last effected. All efforts to move the entire train, were, however of no avail, and the passengers had to be conveyed by an engine attached to a carriage in detachments to Oxford. The first party arriving at about five o'clock in the afternoon.

The 4.45pm up service was also stopped near Radley and remained snow bound all night. A powerful engine was despatched from Oxford and efforts were made to reach the embedded trains, but the engine could not get nearer than 60 yards of the rearmost van of the 4.45 train. A staff of about 200 labourers was sent from Oxford on Wednesday morning to clear the line – a supply of refreshments accompanying them – and after many hours' work their endeavours were successful and the rescued passengers were conveyed to Radley Station. It is worth mentioning the Liddell family that were travelling on the 3.30 down service, as one of their ten children was Alice, who became famous as the inspiration for the book *Alice's Adventures in Wonderland* by Lewis Carroll (Charles Dodgson).

In 1853 the Oxford Worcester and Wolverhampton Railway Company (OW&WR) opened its 89 mile route from Wolverhampton and Worcester through to Oxford. It reached Oxford by way of a junction some three miles north of Oxford at Wolvercote. Agreement had been reached with the Great Western to operate its services from the junction at Wolvercote into Oxford over the existing Great Western lines. The OW&WR had been promoted in 1843, with strong support from the Great Western who actually provided 6 of the 16 directors, basically to counteract the monopoly of the London and Birmingham Railway to the Midlands. The bill to construct the line received Royal Assent on 4 August 1845. With Brunel as its engineer the Great Western probably saw this as a chance to extend the broad gauge northwards from Oxford through to Worcester and Wolverhampton. This did not happen as various clauses were incorporated into the Act which provided for a mixed gauge line to be constructed, and although the broad gauge was built in places, apart from a Board of Trade inspection train the broad gauge was probably never used. The OW&WR could have been a big player in the expansion of the railway locally; unfortunately

Oxford Worcester & Wolverhampton (West Midland Railway) 2-2-2 No. 51 *Will Shakspere*. This was the type of locomotive that worked the early OW&WR services between Wolverhampton, Worcester and Oxford. Built by E. B. Wilson and Co. in 1856, it was withdrawn in December 1878. (Author's Collection)

like many other early proposals it was beset with financial problems from the start. In the OW&WR's case it was due in no small measure to a major error on Brunel's part in substantially underestimating the cost of construction. The prospectus for the railway was issued on 22 May 1844 and put the cost of construction at £1.5 million, but the true cost proved to be around £2.5 million, which resulted in a number of disagreements between the two companies. With money at a premium and with constant disagreement between the OW&WR and the Great Western, delays continued. However, the situation was partially resolved, and the OW&WR together with the contractors Peto and Betts proceeded to try and complete the line themselves.

One of many problems was the delay in the construction of Campden (or Mickelton) Tunnel. This sorry saga has become known as the 'Battle of Mickleton' and although some 40 miles from Oxford it is worth relating the story. Work on the construction of the tunnel was being undertaken by a subcontractor named Robert Marchant, but with heavy clay, together with constant flooding, progress became slow. This lack of progress came to a head in July 1851 when Brunel was instructed by the main contactors Peto and Betts to take over the work. Payments to Marchant ceased so he promptly stopped work and proceeded to barricade his equipment. There are many reports of what happened next but this report from *The Illustrated London News* of 26 July 1851 aptly describes the confrontation between Brunel and Marchant.

At the Worcester end of the tunnel Mr Cowdery (an agent for Peto and Betts) with 200 men from Evesham and Wyre carrying pickaxes and shovels met Marchant who dared them to proceed on pain of being shot. He was carrying several pistols. Mr Brunel, unable to persuade Marchant to move, told Peto and Betts' men to proceed and take a line. A rush was made, and several heads were broken and three men had dislocated shoulders. Marchant and his men left for an hour and returned with three dozen policemen from Gloucester Constabulary, some privates from the Gloucester Infantry and two magistrates who read the Riot Act. Fights had again broken out and several had received broken arms and legs. At 4, Mr Charles Watson of Warwick arrived with 200 men and the Great Western sent a similar number to expel Marchant. The magistrates told Marchant's men to start work and Peto and Betts' men to stop work. Marchant gave in and he adjourned with Mr Brunel to come to some amicable agreement. Whilst they were doing so a small number of navvies again started fighting and one had his little finger bitten off. Eventually Messrs Cubbitt and Stevenson (the railway contractors) acted as arbitrators and work was suspended for a fortnight.

Brunel soon got fed up with the whole enterprise and particularly the abandonment of his broad gauge over the route, and resigned as the OW&WR engineer on 17 March 1852. With work progressing once more the line was opened in stages. The last section comprising a single mixed gauge line was opened between Evesham and Wolvercote Junction on 4 June 1853. At this time there was no mixed gauge track south of Oxford so all OW&WR services terminated at Oxford. The June 1853 timetable shows four services in each direction between Oxford and Dudley, running via Worcester and Kidderminster.

OXFORD, WORCESTER, & WOLVERHAMPTON.

FROM OXFORD. WEEK DAYS. SUN.

Dis Mls.	STATIONS.	1 2 & 3 Class	1 & 2nd Class.	1 & 2nd Class.	1st & 2nd Class.	1st & 2nd Class.	1st & 2nd Class. (Sun.)	1 2 & 3 Class (Sun.)
		A. M	A. M	P. M	P. M.	P. M.	A. M	P. M.
0	Oxford	8 25	11 10	1 20	4 20	6 55	7 30	6 5
7¾	Handborough	8 40	11 30	1 35	4 40	7 15	7 50	6 20
13¾	Charlbury	8 55	11 45	1 50	4 55	..	8 2	6 35
17¼	Ascott	9 0	..	..	5 5	..	8 6	6 46
18¾	Shipton	9 10	..	2 0	5 10	7 40	8 20	6 50
24½	Addlestrop	9 30	..	2 15	5 25	..	8 35	7 5
28¾	Moreton	9 40	12 10	2 25	5 35	7 55	8 47	7 17
32	Blockley	9 48	..	2 35	5 43	..	8 56	7 26
34	Campden	9 55	..	2 40	5 50	..	9 1	7 31
38¾	Honeybourne	10 5	..	..	6 0	..	9 14	7 44
43¼	Evesham	10 15	12 35	3 0	6 10	8 25	9 26	7 55
57¼	Worcester	11 0	1 5	3 40	7 0	8 50	10 0	8 30
80	Dudley	12 25	2 10	5 0	8 20	10 0	11 25	9 50
91	Wolverhampton	12 50	2 25	5 25	..	10 20	11 50	10 10

FROM WOLVERHAMPTON. WEEK DAYS. SUN.

Dis Mls.	STATIONS.	1 & 2nd Class	1 2 & 3 Class	1 & 2nd Class	1st & 2nd Class.	1st & 2nd Class.	1 2 & 3 Class. (Sun.)	1st & 2nd Class. (Sun.)
		A. M.	A. M.	A. M.	P. M	P. M.	A. M.	P. M.
0	Wolverhampton	..	8 0	9 50	1 20	4 20	8 0	4 45
6	Dudley	6 30	8 30	10 25	2 0	4 40	8 30	5 15
33½	Worcester	7 30	9 55	12 0	3 10	5 40	9 55	6 40
47¼	Evesham	8 0	10 25	12 35	3 40	6 10	10 25	7 10
52¼	Honeybourne	..	10 37	12 47	3 50	..	10 37	7 22
57	Campden	..	10 52	1 0	4 5	..	10 50	7 35
59	Blockley	..	10 58	1 5	4 10	..	10 55	7 40
62¼	Moreton	8 30	11 7	1 15	4 18	6 40	11 3	7 48
66½	Addlestrop	..	11 17	1 26	4 28	..	11 15	8 0
72½	Shipton	8 45	11 32	1 35	4 40	6 57	11 30	8 15
73½	Ascott	..	11 37	..	4 45	..	11 35	8 20
77¼	Charlbury	8 55	11 45	1 50	4 55	..	11 45	8 30
83¼	Handborough	9 10	12 0	2 0	5 10	7 15	11 57	8 42
91	Oxford	9 35	12 20	2 20	5 3	7 25	12 15	9 0

Early OW&WR timetable dated April 1854 showing standard gauge services between Oxford and Wolverhampton via Worcester. (Author's Collection)

The inability of the OW&WR to operate south of Oxford was resolved when a standard gauge connection was completed between the OW&WR at Yarnton Junction and the standard gauge LNWR line at Oxford Road Junction on 1 June 1854. The completion of the 1½ mile 'Yarnton Loop' now gave the OW&WR direct access to the LNWR line to Bletchley and Euston and also via a second 'South-west Junction loop' direct access to the LNWR goods yard and station at Oxford Rewley Road. Except for the occasional goods service this second loop saw little use. It was taken out of service in 1861 and removed during 1863. The OW&WR was quick to exploit the Yarnton connection and from 1 April 1854 a new through service between Worcester and Euston was inaugurated, with up to four trains a day making the journey; the fastest time for the 129½ miles being around 4 hours. These services completely avoided Oxford, but between 1854 and 1861 the station at Handborough became important as a junction station; it even had its own refreshment room. Passengers using the Euston to Worcester service could alight here and catch a connecting service to Oxford.

The arrival of the railway obviously had an effect on trade in Oxford. One would assume that it was generally a positive effect, but not it seems for the canal and river trade. Writing in the *Jackson's Oxford Journal* on 22 March 1853 the Reverend Vaughan Thomas summarised the situation:

> Trade, prosperous trade,
> may be said to have taken flight
> from the District, and may be now
> seen in the heavy-goods' train,
> whirling onwards at the rate of
> 12 or 14 miles an hour, whistling in
> derision as it passes by the Thames
> and Canal Navigation, and by its
> speed mocking the drowsy barge
> (that emblem of the old slowness
> of traders, and the torpid course
> of their commercial transactions)
> which would reach the rail train's
> terminus in four or five days and
> nights after it, and then return
> in eight or ten days more, if it
> escaped being grounded on its
> passage home.

True words indeed as the spread of railways throughout the country had

A postcard view of the ex-Oxford, Worcester and Wolverhampton Railway station at Handborough, seen here in the early 1900s. Originally known as Handborough Junction when the OW&WR operated its direct services between Worcester and Euston in 1854. Here trains would connect to the GWR line via Wolvercot Junction and Oxford. A small refreshment room was built at this time to deal with the increased patronage. Its close proximity to Blenheim Palace can be seen on the running-in board. (Author's Collection)

a devastating effect on both river and canal trade.

During December 1856 mixed gauge lines had been opened between Basingstoke, Reading West Junction and Oxford; however it was not until 1861 that the standard gauge was extended between Reading and Paddington. This now gave the West Midland Railway (WMR), as the OW&WR had now become, standard gauge access to London via Oxford. Subsequently, during September 1861 the longer service from Worcester to Euston was discontinued and from 1 October 1861 new standard gauge services were inaugurated between Paddington and Worcester, and Paddington to Wolverhampton and Birkenhead. On Tuesday 1 October the first standard gauge service from Paddington, the

9.35am service to Birmingham and Birkenhead, arrived at Oxford some five minutes late, hauled by Beyer, Peacock 2-2-2 No. 75, built for the GWR in 1856. At Oxford No. 75 was replaced by fellow class member No. 76. Unfortunately the train was further delayed at Leamington when a carriage had to be removed due to a hot box, but with some fine running it reached Birmingham just three minutes late.

One important aspect of the opening of the railway in Oxford was the increase in employment it provided. The railway brought extra trade to the City, which resulted in the growth of many ancillary services such as goods merchants, booking agents and cab companies. From its early days the workforce required to operate the railway locally had gradually increased

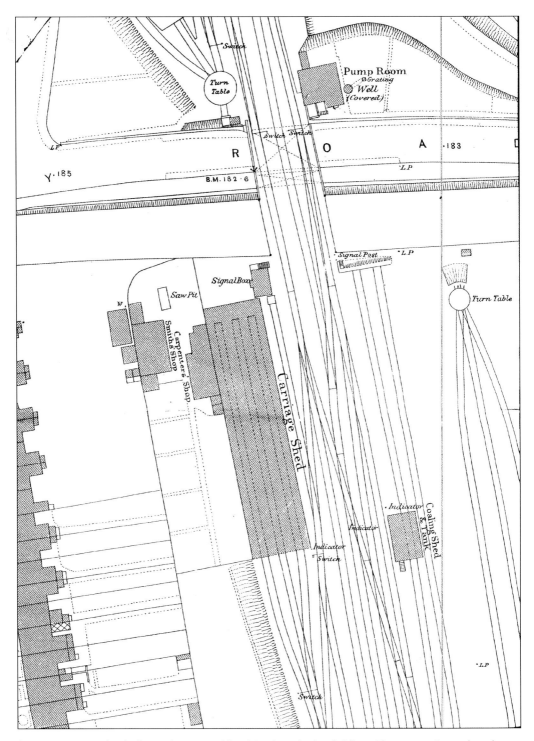

The 1876 OS map clearly shows the West Midland Carriage shed and sidings. These were situated on the down side south of the Botley Road bridge. Notice also the coaling shed and water tank in the Becket Street yard and the wagon turntable at the south end of the down platform. (Ordnance Survey)

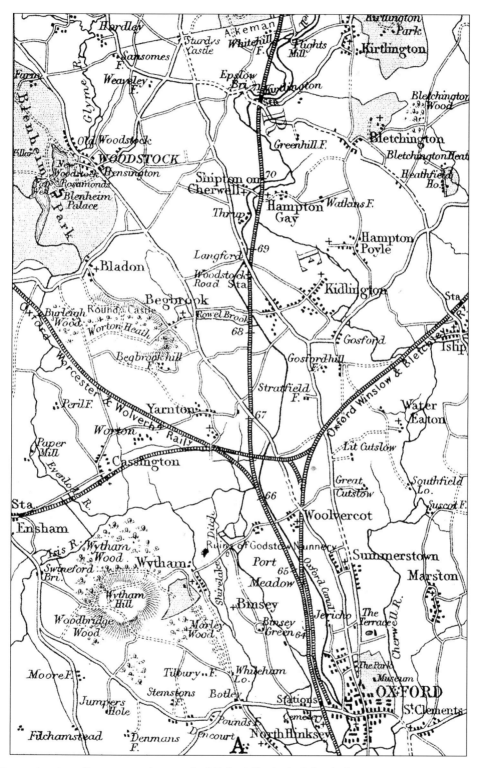

1865 map showing railway connections north of Oxford. (Author's Collection)

from around 100 in 1850, so that by the 1920s there were around 1,500 men and women working for both the GWR and LNWR in the Oxford area. The local areas such as Osney, Grandpont and Jericho became popular residential locations for many of these workers. Interestingly Osney Town was laid out in 1851 by the Oxford Town Clerk, George P. Hester. The houses were extensively constructed to house the influx of railway workers being employed by the two companies. The 1861 census shows that around one third of the inhabitants of Osney Town were listed as railway workers.

The excursion became a major feature of railway operations in this country. This resulted in Oxford becoming a popular destination for tourists, with excursion trains arriving from many areas. *Jackson's Oxford Journal* reported that the first 'experimental' excursion train from Paddington, Slough and Reading to Oxford, comprising 25 carriages, ran on Sunday 18 August 1850, with upwards of 1,600 'excursionists' visiting the City. It went on to report that 'the weather was very favourable, and the excursionists, viewing the various colleges, public buildings, gardens and walks, returned at 7 o'clock, highly delighted with what they had seen in this far-famed University and City.' Oxford soon became an important excursion destination for both the GWR and LNWR. This constant influx of 'excursionists' resulted in the growth of souvenir shops, eating houses and other hostelries.

With the railway firmly established in Oxford, the peace was once again broken when in 1865 the Great Western were looking for a site to build their carriage and wagon works. On 27 April 1865 the Company had approached the council with a proposal to build the new works at Oxford. In an arrangement with the local corporation the GWR had agreed to lease 22 acres of land at Cripley Meadow

for the proposed carriage works site. The GWR apparently favoured the site at Oxford because of its central position and at the time its mixed gauge track. The council were of course interested because of the extra revenue this would bring to the City, as well as the large boost to local employment. At this time the University was (and still is) a powerful force in City affairs and an influential landowner; unfortunately it was immediately against the proposal. Very soon a propaganda war was waged against both the Council and the GWR, with pamphlets being distributed to any parties interested in suppressing the works. One notable article appeared in the London *Times* with the headline 'The GWR Vandals and Oxford'. It was probably an interesting time to be an Oxford resident and to witness yet another fight between the Council and the University (Town and Gown). The University need not have worried as Daniel Gooch, who had been elected as Chairman of the Great Western, made the logical decision to build his carriage and wagon works alongside the locomotive works at Swindon. It seems that this was a purely financial decision and not prompted by the University's objections. The land being offered at Oxford often flooded during the winter months and it would have cost the GWR a considerable amount to alleviate the problem. At Swindon there was no such problem, with no University to object and with the Council eager to increase local employment and the status of the Town. The works were constructed at Swindon at half the cost of constructing them at Oxford. Thus Swindon became a major railway town, leaving the academic tranquillity of Oxford undisturbed.

The introduction of standard gauge services saw the rapid reduction in broad gauge services through Oxford,

GREAT WESTERN RAILWAY

ST. GILES' FAIR.

On MONDAY, SEPTEMBER 3rd, 1883,

A CHEAP TRAIN

FOR

OXFORD

WILL LEAVE					Fares There and Back. THIRD CLASS.	
				A.M.	s.	d.
Wolverhampton (Low Level)	...	...	...	7 45	6	0
Bilston	...	...	...	7 50		
Wednesbury	...	...	...	7 55	5	6
West Bromwich	...	...	...	8 5		
Handsworth	...	...	...	8 10		
Hockley	...	...	...	8 20		
Birmingham (Snow Hill)	...	...	...	8 30	5	0
Bordesley	...	...	...	8 35		
Solihull	...	...	...	8 45		
Knowle	...	...	...	8 55		
Stratford-on-Avon	...	...	8 40	4	6
Hatton	...	...	...	9 15		
Warwick	...	...	...	9 20	4	0
Leamington	...	...	...	9 30		
Southam Road	...	...	...	9 40	3	6
Fenny Compton	...	...	...	9 50	3	0
Cropredy	...	...	...	10 0		
Banbury	...	...	...	10 10	2	6
King's Sutton	...	...	...	10 20		
Aynho	...	...	...	10 30	2	0
Somerton	...	...	...	10 35	1	6
Heyford	...	...	...	10 45		

First Class Tickets issued at Double the above Fares.

Children under 3 years of Age, Free; 3 and under 12, Half-Price.

RETURNING FROM OXFORD THE SAME DAY AS UNDER:—

For Stratford at 8.10 p.m.
For all other Stations at 8.30 p.m.

The Tickets are not transferable, and are only available to and from the Stations named upon them, and by the Trains specified in the Bills; Passengers using them otherwise will be charged the full Ordinary Fare. No Luggage allowed.

PADDINGTON, *August*, 1883. **J. GRIERSON**, *General Manager.*

Waterlow & Sons Limited, Printers, London Wall, London.

Poster advertising St Giles' Fair Oxford 1883. The fair dates from 1625; originally a Parish Festival, it is held on the first Monday and Tuesday following the first Sunday after 1 September which is St Giles' Day. The fair has now evolved to what is essentially a large funfair and is still a major attraction in Oxford. (Author's Collection)

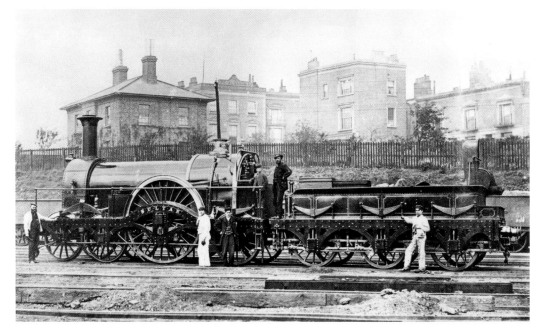

The opening of the line to Birmingham in 1852 saw many of the services operated by Gooch's 'Iron Duke' class 8ft singles. Pictured here at Westbourne Park is Sultan, built in November 1847, it is seen here in its original condition with open cab. These fine locomotives were withdrawn from the Paddington, Oxford and Birmingham services with the removal of the Broad Gauge north of Oxford on 1 November 1868. (Great Western Trust)

A view of the floods at Kennington taken in October 1894. From the opening of the Oxford Railway in 1844 the line has flooded at this point with remarkable regularity. It was not until 2015 that extensive drainage and culvert work was undertaken by Network Rail to alleviate the problem. (Great Western Trust)

THE GREAT WESTERN RAILWAY WORKMEN AND OXFORD.

To the Editor of the " Daily Telegraph."

Sir,—Professor Goldwin Smith, in his letter to the " Daily News," has taken the aristocratic view of this question : allow me, as an Oxford tradesman, to express the plebeian.

He " suspects that the real interests of the City in the matter have been misunderstood." What he intends by the expression " real interests " is somewhat obscure. English tradesmen generally understand their " pecuniary " interests. Oxford tradesmen have given to the matter in question anxious consideration.

He says that the University is to Oxford " its staple and the mainstay of its wealth." The University now acknowledge the principles of free trade : they buy in the cheapest market, and sell in the dearest ; they raise their tenants' rents and demand large discounts from their tradesmen ; if goods can be obtained cheaper from London, from London are they obtained. The City has thus suffered from free trade : it now seeks its advantages, by importing some of the " backbone of England."

He says, " of course the new population will have new shops or co-operative stores of its own." Of this same deprecated co-operative principle the University largely avails itself.

He speaks of the " moral character of Oxford Undergraduates," and of " the danger" from intercommunication " both to the Undergraduates and to the workmen." Strange it is how the point of view can alter opinions. Some hold that one of England's greatest dangers arises from the isolation of classes. Professor Goldwin Smith is well known as an advanced Liberal, a free-trader, a " friend of the working man :" after years of profound study he has arrived at the solemn conviction that *British workmen are not fit to live in the same town with his pupils.*

There is one great advantage which would accrue to the University from such a benighted " new population :" it would afford a fine field for incipient Curates.

He calls Oxford " the casket which holds not unworthily the national memories of a thousand years." One of its greatest charms is its extreme quietness :—

> " The very air seems eloquently fraught
> With the deep silence of devoted thought."

This quietness is to those who have leisure and means, delightful ; but in the midst of this " deep silence" the townspeople find it very difficult to obtain a living, and naturally seek to increase their trade.

The following has, I understand, been set to music, and will be sung at the Commemoration :—

> Hence, loathed British workman,
> Of Great Western Railway born,
> In Paddington forlorn,
> 'Mongst horrid engines, carriages, and trades unholy ;
> Find out some uncouth town,
> Where brooding chimneys spread their noisome smoke,
> And the mighty hammer swings ;
> There under iron roofs, and low-brow'd sheds,
> In dark Cimmerian cities ever dwell !

PLEBEIAN.

June 7, 1865.

Written by J. S. Edgar, formerly assistant to Mr. J. S. Parker, Bookseller.

Letter to the *Daily Telegraph* regarding the proposed construction of the carriage works at Oxford. The letter is signed 'Plebeian' who was subsequently identified as J. S. Edgar, the assistant to J. S. Parker, a local bookseller. (Author's Collection)

and although they continued to run northwards, they rarely ventured north of Leamington. On 1 November 1868 these services ceased north of Oxford when broad gauge working was removed from the timetable, the track being removed during the following year. The era of broad gauge at Oxford was rapidly coming to an end, and by 1870 the only regular broad gauge services comprised goods trains running to and from the goods depot at Grandpont. The end came on 25 November 1872 with the removal of the broad gauge south of Oxford. The goods depot at Grandpont, which had never been converted to standard gauge, was closed on the same day with the land being cleared and sold for housing development.

With the opening of the four local branch lines, to Abingdon in 1856, Witney in 1861, Princes Risborough in 1864 and Woodstock in 1890, rail growth in the area was finally completed. However it was the opening of two new lines, which although not close to Oxford, would have a profound effect on local railway services. The first of these was the 8½ mile Great Western/Great Central connection from Culworth Junction on the Great Central Railway (GCR) to Banbury Junction on the Great Western. The line was opened for goods and mineral traffic on 1 June 1900 and to passengers on 13 August of the same year. This new connection allowed through trains from the north-east direct access to the south via Banbury and Oxford. Whereas this first line resulted in more services travelling through Oxford, the opening of the second line actually reduced the number of services. This was the result of the completion of the new cut-off route between Paddington and Banbury which was achieved with the opening of the section between Ashendon Junction and Aynho on 4 April 1910. The new line provided a much shorter and quicker direct route to Birmingham and beyond, and as a result many of the Paddington to Birmingham services that previously ran via Oxford were diverted to run on the new line.

Chapter 2

THE LNWR AT OXFORD

From its opening in 1851 the 31¼ mile Buckinghamshire Railway branch from Bletchley to Oxford formed an important part of a 77 mile cross-country route for both passenger and freight traffic between Oxford, the LNWR main line at Bletchley, the Midland main line at Bedford and the Great Eastern at Cambridge, the latter being reached in 1872.

The Buckinghamshire Railway Company had been formed in 1844 with the amalgamation of the Buckingham & Brackley Junction Railway and the Oxford & Bletchley Railway. The new Company received Royal Assent in 1847 to construct branches to Oxford and Banbury, running via Verney Junction where the line split, northwards to Banbury and westwards to Oxford. With the full support of the LNWR, and Robert Stephenson as its engineer, construction of the line started in 1847, and with good progress being made the Banbury branch was the first to open on 1 May 1850, followed a year later on 20 May 1851 by the branch to Oxford. Although the construction of the Oxford branch was progressing well it seems that it was not until December 1850 that the Company turned its thoughts to the construction of the Oxford Terminus. The land chosen was the derelict site where once stood Rewley Abbey, a Cistercian monastery founded in around 1287 by Edmund, 2nd Earl of Cornwall. The dissolution of the monasteries by Henry VIII resulted in the closure of the Abbey in 1539.

The following advert regarding the construction of the station appeared in *Jackson's Oxford Journal* dated 7 December 1850:

> To Builders. The Buckinghamshire Railway Company are about to erect a station at their Oxford Terminus. Persons desirous of tendering for the erection of the same are requested to be in attendance at the Engineer's office, Euston Station, at half past one-o'clock on Saturday the Seventh of December next, for the purpose of appointing Surveyors to take out the quantities. By order
>
> Edward Watkin, Secretary. Offices of the Company, Euston Station 19 November 1850.

Interestingly it was initially proposed to construct the terminus building slightly further west with the goods shed being placed to the east between the new station and Rewley Road. However, the Company Directors' minute book of 7 November 1850 states 'that the building be made and placed so as to be capable of expansion without demolitions,' and 'that the positions of Passenger and Goods stations to be reversed so that the passenger station be nearer the Town.'

A further minute dated 12 December 1850 states:

> That in reference to the Central Station at Oxford – Mr Dockray produced plans shewing designs of the permanent buildings both in stone and wood work. Resolved that tenders be obtained for the Oxford station on the plans proposed for the alternatives of wood and stone for the front buildings, and that Fox Henderson & Company be asked to Tender for the whole erection on the plan of the exhibition building, in all respects, as information for the Board.

Robert Benson Dockray (1811–1871) was the Engineer for the LNWR at this time. He had produced his first report regarding the Oxford terminus on 3 June 1850, and it is possible that his work on this was some of his last for the Company, as he resigned from the LNWR due to ill health in early 1852.

With delays in the purchase of the land, it was not until 9 January 1851 that tenders for the work were finally open. Fox, Henderson & Company won the contract with a bid of just £6,552, somewhat lower than the engineer's original estimate of around £8,000, and markedly lower than the highest bid of £12,330. However, as usual with contractors, this bid was tempered with the proviso that if corrugated iron was used instead of wooden boarding for the sides of the passenger shed, that would cost an additional £31, and that it would be the same price to 'warm the offices with hot water', and another £400 if stronger 4lb glass was used. With the acceptance of the Fox, Henderson quote the Company specified that:

> The whole works to be done for £6,552 including 12 months' maintenance, or if corrugated iron be used £31 more. Any alterations to strength, or detail, which Mr Dockray may consider necessary to be made at his request, without increase in cost to the company. The whole to be completed ready for use in 3 months from January 16 instant.

Fox, Henderson & Co were in a good position to win the contract as they were also the engineers of the Crystal Palace, which had been constructed for the Great Exhibition at Hyde Park in 1851. This building was designed by Sir Joseph Paxton and it was his method of construction that was used in the design of the new station at Oxford. This comprised prefabricated cast iron bolt-together sections, a pioneering method of unit building at that time. One of the main differences in construction was that for the station the main structure was bolted together, instead of using Paxton's patented wedge fixing as in the Crystal Palace.

The station provided at Oxford comprised a 450ft long island platform covered by a large glass roofed train shed. At the terminus end the station frontage contained a large entrance hall, booking office and other general offices and amenities. The roof structure was constructed using 24ft span cast iron girders and 48ft span wrought iron trusses, which were supported on cast iron columns similar in style to those used on the Crystal Palace. Initially the overall roof was glazed longitudinally, but in 1888 the roof was extensively rebuilt with the glazed panels running laterally in a standard northlight pattern. Also around 1880 the station was provided with a large circular booking office which also doubled as the Stationmaster's office. It is thought that this structure had previously been in use at the Great Exhibition of 1851, but with no sentiment to the past, it was sadly broken up soon after the station closed in 1951.

A view of the LNWR station at Rewley Road around the turn of the last century. The horse drawn cabs seen here plying for trade had their own separate arrangement with the LNWR and were not allowed to ply for hire at the nearby GW station. (Author's Collection)

The interior of Rewley Road in LNWR days taken sometime after 1909, when the island platform was paved and raised. On the right after arriving with a service from Bletchley is LNWR Webb 1P 2-4-2T No. 413. (Author's Collection)

OXFORD, WINSLOW, and BLETCHLEY.—London and North Western.

Fares.	Up.	Week Days.	Sndys	Down.	Week Days.	Sndys
	Oxford ....dep			Curzou St. Sta.		
Islip				B'm'gm 45 dp		
Bicester				Rugby 45		
Launton				London 12		
Claydon				Bletchley J.dp		
Winslow Junction				Swanbourne		
Swanbourne				Winslow Junction		
Bletchley J.ar				Claydon		
London 45				Launton		
Rugby 42				Bicester		
B'mgm 42				Islip		
				Oxford ....arr		

DAY or RETURN TICKETS issued on a Saturday or Sunday, are available until the following Monday.

BANBURY, BUCKINGHAM, and BLETCHLEY.—London and North Western.

Fares.	Up.	Week Days.	Sun	Down.	Week Days.	Sun
1 cls 2 cls 3 cl		mrn mrn aft aft	aft	Curzon St. Sta.	mrn mrn aft aft	mxx
	Banbury......dep			B'mgm 45 dep		
Farthinghoe......				Rugby p. 45		
Brackley				London p. 42		
Buckingham...				Bletchley Jun. dep		
Winslow Junc				Swanbourne		
Swanbourne				Winslow Junc		
Bletchley Junc.				Buckingham		
London p. 45 a.				Brackley		
Rugby p. 42 „				Farthinghoe		
B'mgm 42 „				Banbury ....arr		

Early timetable of LNWR services, including the Oxford and Banbury branches. (Author's Collection)

The opening of the new station at Rewley Road was reported in the *Jackson's Oxford Journal* of 17 May 1851:

It will be seen, by advertisement in an adjoining column, that this line will be opened from the new station on the Botley Road on Tuesday next, and that on the following Tuesday there will be a cheap excursion train to London. We understand that on Monday 26th the Directors intend giving a celebration of the opening, a grand entertainment at the Star Hotel, for which upwards of 400 invitations will be issued. Captain Winne, the Government Inspector, examined the line yesterday, and expressed himself perfectly satisfied at the manner in which it had been constructed.

A further report on the actual opening states that:

On that morning (Tuesday) the first train, consisting of five carriages, left Oxford at 7.45, and the first train into Oxford arrived at 9.30. A large number of persons were present to witness the arrival and departure of the first trains. The trains at present are, from Oxford, 7.45am, 9.55am, 12.25pm, 3.55pm and 8.25pm: on Sundays 9.55am, 2.25pm. From London, 6.30am, 9.15am, 12.00 noon, 3.30pm, and 5.30pm: on Sundays at 10.00am and 6.00pm. —The excursion train, which was announced last week to leave Oxford on Tuesday next has been altered to Monday, in order to give persons the opportunity of attending the Great Exhibition on the first day of its being open at one shilling.

There were eight intermediate stations on the 31¼ mile line, and these were situated at Islip, Bicester, Launton, Marsh Gibbon & Poundon, Claydon, Verney Junction, Winslow and Swanbourne, all of which apart from Bicester were at the time small villages.

For many years the LNWR operated its own office in Cornmarket Street; its goods agent at this time was one John Pratt. Here you could purchase tickets, and send goods and parcels via the LNWR. The office, pictured here in around 1875, stood adjacent to the stables entrance of the Clarendon Hotel. In 1911 the occupants are listed as Robert Ruffell, Goods Agent and S. C. Thomas, Parcels Agent. The office was closed soon after the First World War and by 1924 it was occupied by George Weeks Confectioners. On the left are the offices of J. Brown, local agent for Anglo-Bavarian Brewery Company, founded at Shepton Mallet in 1872. The brewery closed in 1921. (Minn Collection, Bodleian Library)

A feature of the railway approach to the station at Rewley Road was the swing bridge over the Sheepwash Channel. The channel had been opened by the Canal Company in 1796 and provided a connection between the River Thames, the Castle Mill Stream and the Oxford Canal. The Canal was reached from the Castle Mill Stream via the Isis lock. The Oxford Canal ran from Hawkesbury near Coventry to New Road Wharf, Oxford, *en route* it connected with the Coventry and Ashby canals, the Grand Junction and the Warwick & Napton canals. Work on the 71 mile long Oxford canal started in 1769, and finished when it was opened through to the New Road Wharf on 1 January 1790.

The Sheepwash Channel formed an important and sometimes busy connection between the two waterways.

A view of the station at Rewley Road taken in 1935. The terminus is now branded London Midland and Scottish Railway. The old horse cabs have now been replaced by petrol driven taxis. (Author's Collection)

The station entrance taken from Rewley Road, again in the 1930s. On the left is the Frank Cooper Marmalade Factory, which opened on this site in 1903. Standing in the corner of the station forecourt is the 'Railway Coffee Stall'. This wooden building probably opened in around the early 1920s, and was used over the years as a coffee house, tea rooms and lastly as a burger bar. It was closed and demolished in 2001 to make way for the Said Business School. (Author's Collection)

The Great Western had constructed its line to Banbury at a higher level and was able to cross the channel by way of an overbridge. In July 1850, with construction of the railway underway, the Buckinghamshire Company applied to the Thames Commissioners for 'permission to make a swing bridge, instead of a fixed one, over the Thames near to the proposed station'.

There was good reason for this, as unlike on the nearby Great Western line, a bridge over the channel was not an option as its line into Oxford was constructed almost on the level; there was actually a very slight incline down to the terminus. Stephenson's answer was to design a swing bridge which carried the line over the channel, thus allowing rail access to the new terminus whilst keeping the channel open for navigation. The 73ft long bridge weighed some 85 tons; it was originally constructed of wrought and cast iron with a timber track bed which carried two tracks. It is thought that it was probably rebuilt in around 1872, and again in 1906, when in order to cope with heavier locomotives now being used on the branch, much of the old iron structure

was replaced by steel girders. Over the ensuing years commercial traffic using the channel diminished and the bridge was rarely opened. During 1977 and with rail traffic in and out of the yard diminishing the bridge was reduced to just a single track. It was closed with the closure of the goods yard at Rewley Road on 5 April 1984. The construction by Oxford University of the Said Business School, together with private housing, has left the bridge isolated. At the time of writing it is in poor condition. The swing bridge is a designated 'Scheduled Ancient Monument', and the long term conservation of this bridge will require a lot of thought and money. But hopefully in the not too distant future it will be restored somewhere back to its former glory.

The 1876 Ordnance Survey map shows a small signal box and signal post situated north of the swing bridge on the up side, probably controlling the entrance to the station and yard. This was replaced during 1883 by a larger box that stood to the south of the swing bridge. This box, which contained a 36 lever frame plus one spare, was closed on 31 July 1959 and replaced by a ground frame.

The swing bridge over the Sheepwash Channel looking towards the terminus in 1934. What looks like an early ex-LNWR Webb 0-6-0ST is shunting the yard. (Author's Collection)

Looking down from the Station North Signal Box in 1934 shows the close proximity of the two stations. On the right is the GWR up side carriage sidings and site of the old broad gauge shed, and on the left is the LNWR yard and signal box. (Author's Collection)

It is interesting that the station was always known as Rewley Road as the frontage of the station was actually in Park End Street. The reason being that access to the station entrance was from Rewley Road, which at this time was a short stretch of road that ran at right angles to the station and connected Hollybush Row with Hythe Bridge Street (formerly known as Rewley Lane). Park End Street was laid out in 1771/1772 and derives its name from Park End Colliery in the Forest of Dean. For many years the colliery supplied coal for Oxford to a nearby Canal Wharf, hence the name. The opening of the line brought extra employment into the City; a look at the Census returns for the period show that a large percentage of the staff required, particularly the locomotive crews, came from the Bletchley and Bedford areas. Many set up home in nearby Osney Town.

In around 1890 the LNWR constructed a brick built 'Station House' together with a number of new coal offices that were situated alongside the entrance to the goods yard in Rewley Road. The offices were numbered by the Post Office as 1–12 Rewley Road and were soon taken up by the various coal merchants trading from the adjacent yard. The station house is clearly seen on many photographs of the station area, but in researching its use I can find no evidence of any of the LNWR/LMS Stationmasters actually living there. It was however used in later years by the Great Western and Western Region for temporary staff accommodation. In the 1950s it was for a few years at least the home of Mr Jones, the Oxford locomotive shed foreman.

Up until around 1905 the LNWR Stationmaster's official residence is listed as 'The Elms'. This building together

This interesting but obviously posed picture shows a Bullnose Morris Car and a Tuckwell and Sons Ltd horse wagon in the general goods yard at Rewley Road in around 1925. The large goods shed can be seen on the left. Tuckwell and Sons was a local builders' merchant founded in 1840 by Harold Tuckwell operating from Chappell Street, Oxford. Today the company is still trading and supplies aggregates from its base at Radley. (Author's Collection)

with a large garden was situated opposite the station on the corner between Park End Street and Hollybush Row; it is clearly marked on the 1876 OS map of the area. Its origin probably dates from 1853 when on 2 May of the same year the LNWR signed a 40 year lease with the landowner Christ Church College for 'a plot of land' adjacent to Hollybush Row. The lease does not mention a house, which seems to indicate that it is quite probable that the LNWR built 'The Elms' on this plot as accommodation for the Rewley Road Stationmasters. The LNWR lease on the land ran out in 1893, and in 1902 a large part of the garden and adjacent land that fronted Park End Street was leased by the college to Frank Cooper for the construction of his new marmalade (jam) factory which opened in 1903. Interestingly, the LNWR continued to use 'The Elms'. The last occupant was probably Henry Marshall, as by 1905 the LNWR Stationmasters are shown to be residing in private accommodation. The 1905 Oxford directory lists William Benbow as living in Divinity Road, Cowley. 'The Elms' was probably demolished in the early 1900s to allow for further expansion of the marmalade factory.

LONDON & NORTH WESTERN
RAILWAY.

Commencing on Friday, October 20th,
- - - THE - - -
SERVICE OF TRAINS
BETWEEN
OXFORD AND BICESTER
WILL BE AS UNDER:—

UP.	M	M	M			M	noon	p.m.	p.m.	p.m.	p.m.	M		M	M		Th. & SO M
	a.m.	a.m.	a.m.	a.m.	a.m.	a.m.				p.m.	p.m.	p.m.	p.m.	p.m.	p.m.	p.	p.m.
Oxford	7 15	7 45	9 3	9 45	10 50	11 25	12 0	12 30	12 55	1 50	2 25	4 40	4 50	5 40	6 50	7 28	11 0
Woolvercot	7 21	...	9 9	...	...	11 31	...	...	...	1 56	...	...	4 56	...	6 56	...	11 6
Oxford Road	7 25	...	9 13	...	...	11 35	...	...	...	2 0	...	...	5 0	...	7 0	...	11 10
Islip	7 32	7 57	9 20	9 57	...	11 42	12 12	12 42	...	2 7	2 37	4 51	5 7	...	7 7	7 58	11 16
Oddington	7 37	...	9 24	...	...	11 46	...	...	...	2 11	...	...	5 11	...	7 11	...	11 24
Charlton	7 41	...	9 29	...	...	11 51	...	...	...	2 16	...	...	5 16	...	7 16	...	...
Wendlebury	7 47	...	9 35	...	...	11 57	...	...	...	2 22	...	...	5 22	...	7 22	...	...
Bicester	7 50	8 7	9 40	10 7	11	7 12	2	12 22	12 55	1 12	2 27	2 49	5 1	5 27	5 56	7 27	7 50	11 32

DOWN.	M	M	M			M	p.m.	p.m.	M	p.m.	p.m.	M	M	p.m.	p.m.	Th. & SO M
	a.m.	a.m.	a.m.	a.m.	a.m.	p.m.	p.m.	p.m.	p.m.	p.m.	p.m.	p.m.	p.m.	p.m.	p.m.	p.m.
Bicester	8 0	9 8	9 50	11 2	11 52	12 20	1 15	2 51	3 5	4 9	5 6	5 35	7 45	8 0	9 22	10 34	11 40
Wendlebury	8 4	...	9 55	...	...	12 25	...	...	3 10	...	...	5 40	8 5	...	...	...
Charlton	8 9	...	10 1	...	...	12 31	...	...	3 16	...	...	5 46	8 11	...	...	11 48
Oddington	8 13	...	10 6	...	...	12 36	...	...	3 21	...	...	5 51	8 16	...	...	...
Islip	8 17	9 19	10 10	11 14	...	12 40	1 28	3 3	3 25	...	5 18	5 55	7 57	8 20	10 46	11 56
Oxford Road	8 23	...	10 17	...	...	12 47	...	...	3 32	...	...	6 2	8 27	...	...	12 2
Woolvercot	8 26	...	10 21	...	...	12 51	...	...	3 36	...	...	6 6	8 31	...	...	...
Oxford	8 30	9 30	10 27	11 25	12 10	12 57	1 42	3 15	3 42	4 27	5 30	6 12	8 10	8 37	9 50	11 0	12 10

M—Motor Car—One Class only.

☞ MARKET TICKETS ARE NOT AVAILABLE BY THE MOTOR CAR.

The Fares by the Motor Cars will be as follows:—

	Wendlebury.	Charlton.	Oddington.	Islip.	Oxford Road.	Woolvercot.	Oxford.
	d.	d.	d.	d.	d.	d.	s. d.
Bicester	1	3	4	6	8	9	1 0
Wendlebury	...	2	3	4	6	8	0 10
Charlton	2	...	1	2	4	6	0 8
Oddington	3	1	...	1	3	4	0 6
Islip	4	2	1	...	2	3	0 6
Oxford Road	6	4	3	2	...	1	0 3
Woolvercot	8	6	4	3	1	...	0 2
Oxford	10	8	6	6	3	2	...

PARCEL TRAFFIC will be dealt with at OXFORD, ISLIP, ODDINGTON, WENDLEBURY, and BICESTER.

Timetable for the new LNWR steam Railmotor services between Oxford and Bicester, dated 20 October 1905. (Author's Collection)

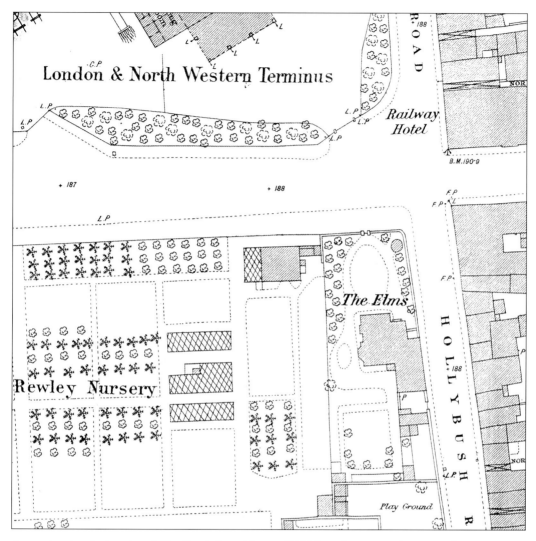

A map showing the location of 'The Elms', the residence of LNWR stationmasters from around 1854 until 1899. (Ordnance Survey)

The following list of LNWR/LMS Stationmasters has been compiled using various trade directories as well as local census returns for the St Thomas area. From 1933 the Great Western Stationmaster at Oxford also became responsible for Rewley Road.

Alfred Denny Blott 1851–1862
Frank Stanbury 1862–1871
Thomas Bell Dixon 1871–1881
Thomas Hyatt 1881–1889
William H. Wilkins 1889–1899

Henry Marshall 1899–1905
William Benbow 1905–1921
Thomas Smith 1921–1931
Frederick J. Sharpe 1931–1933
Francis Herbert Buckingham 1933–1941
(also GWR Stationmaster)
Frank C. Price 1941–1951
James Miller 1951–1962
Charles W. Swancote 1962–1964

The withdrawal of the early type of low six-wheeled coaches from the branch in 1909 allowed the island platform at

A 1920s view of LNWR Webb Precedent Class 2-4-0 No. 1668 *Dagmar* as it passes the Railmotor halt at Port Meadow with a service to Oxford. The halt was closed on 25 October 1926. (Author's Collection)

Oxford Road Junction pictured in 1925, with a goods service to Bletchley leaving the Yarnton loop. On the left is the crossing keeper's cottage and on the right Oxford Road Junction signal box, which had opened in February 1876. The main (now A4260) road to Banbury crossed the railway at this point; the crossing was closed and replaced by a new road overbridge in 1935. The signal box was replaced in 1956 and renamed Banbury Road Junction. The Yarnton loop was closed on 8 November 1965. (Author's Collection)

Rewley Road to be paved and raised to the standard height of 36 inches. It is interesting to note that of the intermediate stations on the branch, only Bicester, Marsh Gibbon, Verney Junction and Winslow had their platforms raised. The others retained their low platforms right up until closure, including the Oxford branch platforms at Bletchley. The Grouping of the railways in 1923 saw the station and line became part of the newly formed London Midland and Scottish Railway, and as already mentioned, in 1933 both the Rewley Road passenger and goods departments were placed under the control of the nearby Great Western Stationmaster. A major change took place when in November 1940 a new junction was opened between the GW line and the ex-LNWR line at Oxford North Junction. The new junction was mainly used for freight traffic, but from 1 October 1951 the station at Rewley Road was closed to passenger services, and from that date all passenger services to and from Bletchley

and Cambridge ran via North Junction to the up and down bay platforms at the adjacent Western Region station.

The complete station structure survived pretty much intact right up until closure, and for a number of years afterwards the main station building was used as a railway hostel. It was during this time that nine bays of the train shed roof together with the platform were removed. However, because of its grade two listed status, two of these bays were placed into store by the Science Museum. The railway hostel closed in the mid 1960s after which the building was taken over by a local tyre company. During this period the goods yard at Rewley Road remained open, serving a declining number of coal merchants, a Shell Mex depot and the local stone merchant Axtell & Perry, who were the last occupants of the yard when it closed on 5 April 1984. The few remaining sidings were removed during March 1985; the old station house and coal offices in Rewley Road had previously been demolished

The new road overbridge at Oxford Road Junction under construction in September 1935. (Author's Collection)

A two coach Bletchley to Oxford service hauled by Bowen-Cooke Prince of Wales Class 4-6-0 No. 25683 *Falaba* near Claydon on 13 May 1939. This class of locomotive were regular performers on Oxford Branch services at this time. Built in April 1916, No. 25683 was withdrawn from Bletchley in January 1946. (Author's Collection)

during April/May 1983. During this time much of the yard was being used as a car park for the nearby BR station. The whole area had become something of an eyesore and in December 1999 Oxford University, who owned the land, decided to construct the Said Business School on the site. The old station building, which was and still is Grade 2 listed, was carefully dismantled, and with financial assistance from the Heritage Lottery Fund and Oxford University the old station was moved piece by piece to the Buckinghamshire Railway Centre at Quainton Road where it was carefully reconstructed and fully restored. It was opened as a visitor attraction in 2002. Another piece of history that was removed at the same time was the Station Coffee House.

Today, apart from the swing bridge, any evidence of the LNWR station at Oxford has gone, but a brass plaque commemorating the station has been set in the pavement in what is now Frideswides Square, and adjacent to where the station once stood.

Passenger Services

Passenger services from Rewley Road to Bletchley were from the start mostly semi-fast with trains stopping at each of the eight intermediate stations. Early timetables show six trains each weekday in each direction, which by the turn of the last century had increased to eight, and now included a through service to Bedford and Cambridge. The timetables give an average journey time of around 63 minutes between Oxford and Bletchley and 2hr 12minutes on the direct service to Cambridge. Most of the services connected at Bletchley with fast trains to the North West and London.

On 9 October 1905 the LNWR introduced a steam Railmotor service between Oxford and Bicester with intermediate halts being opened on the same date at Wolvercote, Oxford Road (for Kidlington), Oddington, Charlton and Wendlebury; an additional halt at Port Meadow was opened later on 20 August 1906. Apart from Port Meadow and Wolvercote, photographs indicate that the rest of the halts were at ground level. The service was moderately successful, and apart from the withdrawal of services due to wartime austerity between 1 January 1917 and 5 May 1919, they operated until 25 October 1926 when the service was withdrawn and all of the halts closed.

During the Second World War the line gained extra importance for conveying staff from Oxford and Cambridge to Station X, the top secret code breaking establishment at Bletchley Park. The opening of the Ordnance depot at Bicester during the war, together with the construction of a marshalling yard at Swanbourne in 1941, increased the frequency of both freight and passenger traffic over the line. A regular feature of wartime Oxford were the 'Saturday Night Specials' that brought service personnel direct from the Ordnance Depot for a night out in Oxford. After the war the Great Western took control of the branch as far as Bicester, and for many years ran a special morning and evening workman's service from Oxford and over the MOD lines to and from Piddington. During the latter years of the branch, passenger services comprised eight trains a day in each direction, including one afternoon through service to Cambridge. There were also extra services on Saturdays to and from Bletchley, and two services in each direction on Sundays. In 1959 steam was gradually replaced on passenger services by two-car DMUs. The introduction of the DMUs resulted in the service between Oxford and Cambridge being increased to four through trains each day. Like many other branches there was little if any growth in passenger traffic and

Ivatt LMS Class 4 No. 3000 waits to depart from Rewley Road with a service to Bletchley on 18 October 1948. Six of these locos were allocated to Bletchley from new and operated the Oxford branch services until early 1950. (Mark Yarwood)

After the closure of Rewley Road, passenger services ran to and from Oxford General via Oxford North Junction. On 8 September 1954 ex-Midland 0-6-0 No. 43785 crosses the junction with the 5.18pm through service to Bedford. (Dr G. D. Parks)

subsequently the line was earmarked for closure. As was usual at this time, the large number of complaints regarding the closure of the branch fell on deaf ears and accordingly the last passenger service departed from Oxford to Bletchley at 22.50 on 30 December 1967. However, the branch continued to be used for the occasional goods and parcels traffic, a feature being the weekly empty carriage stock train that ran from Old Oak Common to Wolverton carriage works. I can remember on many occasions this service being hauled by a Western Class diesel hydraulic. Another important service that traversed the branch was the daily compacted waste service from Bristol and Bath to the Calvert brickworks quarry. Introduced during the 1980s the 'binliner' service required a reversal via the connecting spur at Calvert. This spur had been opened on 14 September 1940 and connected the Bletchley line to the ex-Great Central line at Calvert.

At Calvert the waste was unloaded and tipped into the brickworks quarry. I can well remember a cab ride from Oxford to Calvert in 1986 hauled by a Class 56 locomotive; on arrival a good breakfast was had by all at the nearby brick works canteen, followed by a trip to the tip. My abiding memory was of the thousands of seagulls scavenging for food as each container was emptied. The brickworks at Calvert were closed in 1991.

In retrospect, to close such an important cross-country route not just to passenger services but more importantly to freight traffic was at the time a major error. Rationalisation took place between 7 and 29 October 1973 when the wartime junction at Oxford North was removed and replaced by a new single line junction approximately ½ mile further north at milepost 64½. At the same time the line between the new junction and Bicester was singled, followed by the section between Bicester and Clayton in June 1985.

Ex-LNER B12 4-6-0 No. 61546 waits to depart from the down bay at Oxford with the 2.28pm through service to Cambridge on 23 April 1959. (J. D. Edwards)

After the closure of Oxford Rewley Road, passenger services from Bletchley and beyond arrived and departed from the up and down bay platforms. Standing in the up bay in May 1960 is Stanier 2-6-4T No. 42106 with the 09.35am service from Bletchley. (Author's Collection)

Goods Services

One aspect of the branch was the many brickworks that were established along the route between Calvert and Bedford. Brick traffic became an important part of freight working over the branch; these services ran on a regular basis from the various works via the Yarnton Loop to a number of westward destinations. The subsequent switch from rail to road transport during the 1950s, together with the demise of many of the brickworks, saw the subsequent disappearance of these workings.

Very soon after the station was opened a large wooden goods shed was constructed on the Botley Road side of the station. This was served by five sidings, one of which served a loading platform inside the shed. At the Botley Road end a small brick house was constructed, probably around the early 1900s, to house the Goods Superintendent. In later years it is described as 'Station Cottage' and was used, for a number of years, as a hostel for footplate staff. There were also four coal and general merchandise sidings on the east side, adjacent to the Castle Mill Steam and the Rewley Road. For many years, until the opening of Oxford

A great view of the ex-LNWR goods shed at Rewley Road taken in 1958 from the roof of the old Frank Cooper's Marmalade Factory. One of the small buildings in the yard is occupied by A. E. Robson Ltd who were meat cartage contractors. In the foreground is the roof of the Railway Coffee Stall. It was opened around the early 1920s as coffee house and later tea rooms. It remained in use as a cafe and burger bar right up until 2001 when it was closed and demolished to make way for the new Business School. (J. D. Edwards)

North Junction, the only connection to the nearby GWR lines were a couple of exchange sidings just to the north of the swing bridge. Coal was an important commodity and during the nineteenth and early twentieth centuries much of Oxford's coal supplies arrived at Rewley Road for subsequent distribution. Prior to the opening of the line much of the coal traffic came into the city via the Oxford Canal to the Canal basin at New Road. The opening of the railway resulted in a sharp decline of coal traffic arriving at Oxford via the Canal. The 1861 trade directory shows that a number of the coal merchants were still trading from their main offices at the Canal Wharf, but were by now using the coal yard at Rewley Road for their deliveries. Those listed as relocating to Rewley Road were: T. C. Archer, W. Beale, T. Benwell, Gould & Burrell, and R. W. Soanes. The 1876 map shows a number of coal merchant's huts scattered around the yard, and in around 1890 the LNWR 'tidied up' the area with the construction of a number of brick built coal offices in the yard alongside the Rewley Road. With the increase of coal consumption during the period after the First World War, two additional coal sidings were constructed in the yard and two others were extended. The old Canal basin at New Road, which by the 1930s was little used, was purchased in 1937 by Lord Nuffield and subsequently filled in for the construction of Nuffield College. The College, which was not finally completed until 1960, now covers much of the site. The site of the old goods and coal wharf, which is also owned by Nuffield College, has also been filled in and is currently in use as a car park.

The 1911 trade directory shows the following merchants trading from Rewley Road: William Simmonds, William Perkins, Soanes & Taylor, Edwin Welford & Son, Wonnacot Bros, Stevens & Co, and Daniel Symes. Three others, Arthur David, Joseph Green and Gould & Son, are shown as trading from the Great Western Coal Wharf. In 1954 the following merchants are listed as trading at Rewley Road (the numbers relate to the official Rewley Road postal address for each company):

No. 1 – William Simmonds & Son
Nos. 2/3 – George Dunlop & Son
Nos. 4/5 – Ernest Welford and Son
No. 6 – John E. Howkins & Son
No.7 – Bernard T. Frost
Nos. 8/9/10/11/12 – Stevco Ltd

EVENING EXCURSIONS

TUESDAYS   THURSDAYS

FRIDAYS and SATURDAYS

1st JANUARY 1952

UNTIL FURTHER NOTICE

TO

OXFORD

(General Station)

FROM

	Third Class Return Fare		Third Class Return Fare
BICESTER -	1/3	CLAYDON -	2/3
BLETCHLEY	3/3	WINSLOW -	2/6

CHILDREN under three years of age, free; three years and under fourteen, half-fares.

OUTWARD				RETURN Same Day
	p m			p m
Depart	5 5	BLETCHLEY	Arrive	11 43
"	5 22	WINSLOW	"	11 28
"	5 31	CLAYDON	"	11 19
"	5 50	BICESTER (London Road)	"	11 3
Arrive	6 12	OXFORD (General)	Depart	10 40

TICKETS CAN BE OBTAINED IN ADVANCE AT STATIONS AND AGENCIES.

CONDITIONS OF ISSUE

Day, Half-day and Evening tickets are issued subject to the conditions applicable to tickets of these descriptions as shown in the Bye-Laws and Regulations, General Notices, Regulations and Conditions exhibited at stations, or where not so exhibited, copies can be obtained free of charge at the station booking office.

For LUGGAGE ALLOWANCES also see these Regulations and Conditions.

Further information will be supplied on application to Stations, Agencies, or to W. N. ROBERTS, District Passenger Superintendent, Euston House, London, N.W.1. (Telephone: Euston 1234); N. H. BRIANT, District Operating Superintendent, Paddington Station, W.2; or C. FURBER, Commercial Superintendent, Paddington Station, W.2. (Telephone: Paddington 7000. Extn. "Enquiries": 8.0 am to 10.0 pm).

BRITISH RAILWAYS

Published by the Railway Executive (London Midland Region)   B.R. 35000
C7/R (EVEX.) DECEMBER, 1951   Printed by the Carlton Press, Chesham

Evening excursions from Bletchley to Oxford, January 1952. (Author's Collection)

Many goods services by-passed Oxford via the junction at Yarnton. Pictured here is Franco Crosti BR 9F 2-10-0 No. 92029 as it stands in the yard at Yarnton on 11 May 1957. (Author's Collection)

Another cross-country goods service, ex-LNER Class K3 2-6-0 No. 61817 with a goods service from Severn Tunnel Junction to Cambridge joins the Oxford to Bletchley line at Banbury Road Junction. The signal box here opened in November 1956 as Oxford Road Junction. It replaced an earlier box that controlled the level crossing. In September 1958 it was renamed Banbury Road Junction, and closed in October 1973. (J. D. Edwards)

TO AND FROM L.M.R. AT YARNTON

Time Depart	From Yarnton to	Days run	Load	W.R. Feeding Service
1.15 a.m. ...	Saffron Lane Junction ...	Tuesdays to Saturdays ...	Empties ...	—
1.15 a.m. ...	Fletton's Siding	Sundays	Empties ...	
3.20 a.m. ...	Blisworth	Sundays	Empties ...	3.20 p.m. Rogerstone (SO).
3. 0 a.m. ...	Irthlingboro'	Tuesday to Saturdays ...	Empties ...	2.45 p.m. Rogerstone.
7.55 a.m. ...	Swanbourne Sidings ...	Weekdays	Goods ...	7.40 p.m. Pontypool Road
10.15 a.m. ...	Swanbourne Sidings ...	Weekdays	Goods ...	—
11. 0 a.m. ...	Cambridge	Mondays to Saturdays ...	Goods ...	2.30 p.m. Severn Tunnel Jn.
7.45 p.m. ...	Swanbourne Sidings ...	Weekdays	Empties ...	—
8.45 p.m. ...	Northampton	Saturdays	Goods ...	4.35 a.m. Pontypool Road
9.30 p.m. ...	Northampton	Mondays to Fridays	Goods ...	4.35 a.m. Pontypool Road
11.45 p.m. ...	Cambridge	Mondays to Saturdays ...	Goods	12.10 p.m. Llandilo Jn.

Train		Time Due	Days Run	W.R. Connection Yarnton to
Time	From			
9.50 a.m.	Cambridge	1.45 p.m.	Mondays to Saturdays	3.35 p.m. Cardiff
6.10 a.m.	Wellingboro' SX	3.40 p.m.	Mondays to Fridays	4.35 p.m. Honeybourne
11.40 a.m.	Irthlingboro'	5. 0 p.m.	Tuesdays to Saturdays	6.45 p.m. Honeybourne
4‖ 0 p.m.	Bletchley M.P.D. MO ...	5.23 p.m.	Mondays	—
2. 0 p.m.	Irthlingboro' MX ...	7.30 p.m.	Tuesdays to Fridays	11.55 p.m. Honeybourne SX
				11.35 p.m. Honeybourne SO

The **1959** Western Region freight train working timetable showing goods operations to and from the London Midland Region at Yarnton Junction. (Author's Collection)

The LNWR Locomotive Shed

The Buckingham Railway arrived in Oxford with the opening of its terminus at Rewley Road on 20 May 1851. At Rewley Road the Company constructed a small locomotive shed a few hundred yards to the north of the new terminus and the Sheepwash Channel. The shed comprised a three-road through shed with a large workshop on the east side of the building. The whole building measured about 95ft in length and 62ft wide. Just to the south stood a large 16,000 gallon water tank and pump house. The tank was supported on cast iron columns and girders that were similar in style to the new station, and the tower was filled from the nearby River Thames via a steam pump. In the yard was a 42ft diameter turntable. Interestingly, for the whole of its working life the shed was provided with rudimentary coaling facilities, comprising a wooden coaling platform and hand crane. The three-road shed provided accommodation for up to nine locomotives, quite a large number, as in 1855 it was reported that some five locomotives were required to work the branch, with two more in reserve. However, it is quite likely that the extra provision was for the large amount of excursion traffic that came into Oxford. The shed was always a sub-shed of Bletchley and was given the code 4 by the LNWR; some years later it was numbered 30 on the list of LNWR depots.

On 14 October 1877 severe gales demolished part of the shed roof. This was subsequently repaired but on 15 June 1879 part of the workshop and shed roof were destroyed by fire; again repairs were undertaken, but it was not long before a decision was taken to replace the old shed with a more substantial structure. Accordingly, in 1883 the old shed was demolished and a new brick built shed was constructed on the same site. The new shed was a two-road standard Webb northlight pattern dead end shed. It measured some 150ft in length, but being just a two-road shed it was smaller than the old shed, and now held just six locomotives. The shed offices and a small workshop were situated at the north end of the building, the original water tank and turntable being retained, as were the basic coaling facilities. In 1928 the turntable was removed and replaced by a new 50ft turntable, thus allowing larger locomotives to use the branch. The cost of

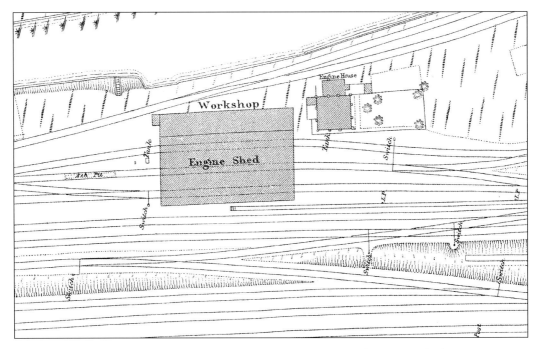

An **1876** map showing the layout of the first three-road LNWR shed at Oxford. It was rebuilt in 1883 into a two-road shed. (Ordnance Survey)

the replacement shed was put at £1,817. Interestingly, it was not until March 1950 that a cover was provided for the coaling platform, a pointless exercise as the shed was closed on 3 December 1950. The closure of the shed saw locomotive servicing together with the remaining staff move to the adjacent ex-Great Western depot. The turntable was soon removed but the empty shed building and water tower stood unused and derelict for some 10 years. The water tower was removed in August 1960, followed by the engine shed in April 1964, after which the site lay empty. In recent years it has been covered by a large development of town houses.

In the early years of the last century services were in the hands of Lady of the Lake Class 2-2-2s and Webb IF Class 0-6-2Ts, the latter continuing on the line until the 1940s. Amongst other locomotives used over the early years of the last century on both branch passenger and excursion trains were members of the George the Fifth, Renown and Precursor Class 4-4-0s,

2-4-0 Precedents, and Experiment and Prince of Wales Class 4-6-0s.

Interestingly the wartime 'Saturday Night Specials' that I have already mentioned were hauled by War Department locomotives comprising a couple of ex-Great Western Dean Goods 0-6-0s together with ex-LSWR Adams Jubilee Class 0-4-2 No. 625.

Through services from Bedford and Cambridge brought in a succession of Midland locomotives such as Johnson and Deeley 0-6-0 and 4-4-0s. After the war passenger services over the branch were mainly in the hands of Stanier 2-6-4Ts. In fact the very last passenger train to leave Rewley Road on 1 October 1951 was hauled by 2-6-4T No. 42667. The introduction during the 1950s of BR Standard Class locomotives saw BR Standard Class 4 2-6-4Ts and 4-6-0s gradually take over the services. The Cambridge services were often worked by Eastern Region D16 Class 4-4-0s, B1 Class 4-6-0s, K3 Class 2-6-0s, and B12 4-6-0s.

A view of the later two-road shed in around 1930. Ex-LNWR Webb 2-4-2T No. 6708 stands in the shed yard. Notice the wooden doors; these were removed prior to the Second World War. (Author's Collection)

A line up of ex-LNWR Whale 4-6-0 locomotives at Oxford on Sunday 3 July 1932. They had worked in previously on excursions, and have been turned and serviced in preparation for their return journey. The front two are identified as Nos. 8813 and 8815. (E. Eggleton)

Whale LNWR Experiment Class 4-6-0 No. 5525 *Byzantium* only just fits on the 50ft turntable at Oxford. This was installed in 1928, and replaced the original 42ft turntable. (Author's Collection)

The two-road locomotive shed taken from a passing troop train on Friday 15 May 1942. In the yard is ex-LNWR Bowen Cooke 0-8-0 No. 8943. (Lt Ted Wurm)

The closed and disused engine shed and water tower at Rewley Road in 1959. The water tower was deemed to be unsafe and was demolished in 1960, followed by the engine shed in 1962. (J. D. Edwards)

The Chiltern Revival

What is known locally as the 'Chiltern Revival' has had a major impact in railway operations at Oxford. The 'revival' of part of the old LNWR route between Oxford and Bicester can be traced back to the formation of Network South East on 12 June 1986. Once established, the new sector decided to introduce an experimental passenger service between Oxford and Bicester. This was relatively straightforward as the single track was still in use for freight services to and from Bicester MOD, together with a daily 'Avon' waste train from Bristol and Bath to Calvert. The old station at Bicester London Road was spruced up and on 9 May 1987 a passenger service was introduced between Oxford and Bicester.

Introducing it as an experimental service meant that if passenger numbers were not forthcoming the Company could withdraw the service without a closure process. However, the service proved to be extremely popular, and two years later on 13 May 1989 a new station was opened at Islip. On 1 April 1994 Network South East was disbanded prior to the privatisation of the railways. Its services in the Thames Valley were taken over from 13 October 1996 by 'Thames Trains', who continued to operate the Bicester services. Yet another change took place on 1 April 2004 when 'Thames Trains' which was part of the Go-Ahead Group merged with the First Group to form 'First Great Western'. Using the new Class 165 Turbo units, the First Group continued to operate the services until May 2011, when the services were taken over by Chiltern Railways. This required a Chiltern Class 165 unit running down from Banbury to Oxford each day to operate the services.

Under project Evergreen, the whole of the section between Oxford and Bicester was upgraded with double-track throughout and more importantly a new junction (chord) was constructed at Bicester to connect with the higher level Chiltern Railways' main line from Marylebone to Birmingham. This allowed through services between Oxford and Marylebone. The first part of the new line opened between Marylebone and a new station at Oxford Parkway on 25 October 2015, with services being extended through to Oxford on 11 December 2016. The new line was the first new rail link to open between a major British city and London in over 100 years. To accommodate the service,

new platforms were constructed at Oxford, together with completely new stations at Islip and at Bicester London Road (now named Bicester Village after the adjacent outlet shopping centre). In 2018 the temporary single line working at Oxford North Junction was removed, with the introduction of the new signalling system in the area. The new line provides an alternative and fast route to London. Since opening it has become very busy; in October 2018 the *Oxford Mail* reported that some 7 million journeys had been made since opening, with 4.5 million travelling to and from Bicester Village, and 2.5 million through Oxford Parkway. At the time of writing the services comprise 37 down and 41 up services each weekday, operating what is essentially a half-hourly service between Oxford and Marylebone. Motive power comprises Chiltern Class 165, Class 168 and 172 DMUs, with one

BR Standard Class 5 No. 73038 from Bletchley hauls the weekly empty stock train from Old Oak Common to Wolverton on the ex-LNWR line at Port Meadow. The stock was being taken to the carriage works for refurbishment. (A. E. Doyle)

An English Electric Class 40 'No. D341' on a long mixed freight to Bletchley passes Aristotle Lane north of Oxford on 5 June 1965. (A. E. Doyle)

Two-car Cravens DMU No. 50394 waits in the down bay on Saturday 30 December 1967 with the 2.55pm passenger service to Bletchley and Cambridge, the last day of passenger operation on the branch. (David Green)

The small station at Islip pictured here in April 1967 with a two-car Derby Unit waiting to depart on a service to Bletchley and Cambridge. On the left are the sidings that served the wartime fuel store. (David Green)

early morning up and one down evening service hauled using a Class 68 locomotive and main line coaching stock. Bicester Village has today become very popular with shoppers, particularly from the Far East, with many arriving by train. On the approach to the station passengers are greeted with on-train announcements in English, Mandarin and Arabic.

The next development of the route will see the reinstatement of services between Oxford and Bletchley and the upgrade of the existing line between Bletchley and Bedford. The 'East West Route' as it is known is being constructed by the East West Railway Company, using both Government and private funding. On 4 October 2018 preliminary work started in preparation for the construction of a double-track railway from Bicester Junction through to Bletchley. The timeline is to open the first section by 2023 and the final section between Bedford and Cambridge by 2030. The section between Oxford and Bedford has been estimated to cost some £270 million, with a total of £530 million for the whole route. Once again the question must be asked, for such an important route, why was it closed in the first place?

The LCGB 'Isis' railtour comprising units W50679, 59271 and 50727, pictured here at Bicester on 14 February 1970. The special was from Bristol to Bristol taking in many of the local branch lines. (Author's Collection)

The ex-LNWR station at Rewley Road in its final use as a Tyre Depot. (Author)

The site of Rewley Road is now covered by the Said Business School; a small plaque set into the pavement is all that commemorates the old station. (Author)

On 9 May 1987 Network South East reintroduced a passenger service between Oxford and Bicester. Seen here passing the site of the Grain Silo and the new Parkway Station at Kidlington is the inaugural service, complete with headboard. (A. E. Doyle)

The new service between Oxford Parkway and Marylebone was introduced on Monday 25 October 2015. On the previous day Chiltern Trains ran a special service over the line, seen here at Oxford Parkway hauled by Chiltern Class 68 No. 68014. (A. E. Doyle)

The new Chiltern line Platforms 1 and 2 at Oxford and the new train crew and staff building were constructed on the site of the up bay and adjacent sidings. Class 168 No. 168005 waits to depart with the 08.40am service to Marylebone on 15 August 2018. The Class 165 No. 165101 will form the 09.06 service to Didcot. This service uses platform 1 as a run round facility to gain entry to the up carriage sidings. (Author)

The remains of the ex-LNWR swing bridge pictured here on 11 June 2018. The bridge is currently in poor condition but the Oxford Preservation Trust are hoping to restore it in the not too distant future. A Marylebone to Oxford service is seen arriving on the higher level ex-Great Western line. (Author)

A Chiltern Railway Class 168 No. 168327 arrives at Bicester Village with a service to Oxford on 11 June 2018. The new station was opened by Chiltern Railways on 25 October 2015. The station is incredibly busy with shoppers travelling to the nearby outlet centre. (Author)

The new station at Bicester Village is provided with two separate ticket barriers, one for the town and the one pictured here direct into the shopping outlet. In the background are the guest services area and a meet and greet service. (Author)

Chapter 3

THE GREAT WESTERN STATIONS

The 1844 Station

As already mentioned the Oxford branch opened from Didcot to Oxford on Wednesday 12 June 1844. The new terminus was situated south of the River Thames (known as the Isis at this point) in the Parish of St Aldates in an area known as Grandpont. The station was constructed of wood and comprised staggered up and down platforms, each partially covered by an overall roof supported on cast iron pillars. An early map shows that the station and yard were served by five lines; two of these terminated at the up platform, one of which was probably a carriage siding, with each being provided with a small turntable. A further two lines served the down platform and a large wooden goods shed, which was situated alongside the down platform. Another line passed between both the down platform and goods shed and continued for about 400 yards to terminate at a small wharf alongside the River Isis. The track plan shows that the goods shed and the down platform lines connected with this long siding just to the north of the down platform, thus forming a run around facility. With the main locomotive servicing facilities being provided at Didcot, only basic services were provided at Oxford. These comprised a locomotive turntable, a small wooden coal stage, and a water tank (which apparently was still

in situ long after the station closed) which was filled with water from the nearby River Thames. I can find no reference to the first Stationmaster as such but James Kelley is listed as being the Station Inspector in 1846. The station was accessed from the nearby Abingdon Road via a lane which is shown on the map as 'leading to the Great Western Station', and not, as is commonly thought, the current Western Road, which was not constructed or named until 1880.

The long siding to the Isis goods wharf is mentioned in the 19 September 1846 edition of *Jackson's Oxford Journal* when it reported that 'on Saturday last two porters employed by the Great Western at Oxford, Isaac Batts and James Gardener, were killed whilst unloading timber at the wharf.' It goes on to say:

> It appears that these two men with six others were employed in hoisting with a crane two large trees that were floating in the River Isis, adjoining, and which were to be conveyed by rail. The men had succeeded in raising one tree and placing it on the truck, and were about to raise the second, when, in spite of their combined efforts to swing it in the direction they required, it suddenly rebounded and striking with great force a portion of the crane, the shaft was driven out of its position and the

supports gave way and the whole fell to pieces. The porters hearing a crash endeavoured to get out of the way, and all succeeded in doing so except Batts and Gardener.

Their bodies were taken to the nearby Elephant & Castle public house in St Aldates to await the coroner's inquest which was held on the Monday. The verdict was accidental death. Batts was buried in his home village of Southleigh and Gardener at St Thomas Church, Oxford, the Great Western defraying the costs of each funeral. This was the first recorded fatality on the railway at Oxford.

On 2 September 1850 the Great Western opened its 24½ mile single-track broad gauge line from Oxford through to Banbury. Trains travelling over the route were required to reverse at Millstream Junction to gain access to the station at Grandpont. Provision had been made for doubling of the track and this was undertaken as the line was extended northwards to Birmingham. Soon after the Banbury section was opened, work was started on the construction of a new station further north and adjacent to what is now the Botley Road, which in the nineteenth century was apparently known as Seven Bridges Road. *Jackson's Oxford Journal* reported in December 1851 that the new station was under construction and was partially open for services to Banbury, with four down trains each day calling there. It does not mention any up services so it is probable that only the down side was being used at this time. This report is interesting as it suggests that for several months both the old and new stations were in use.

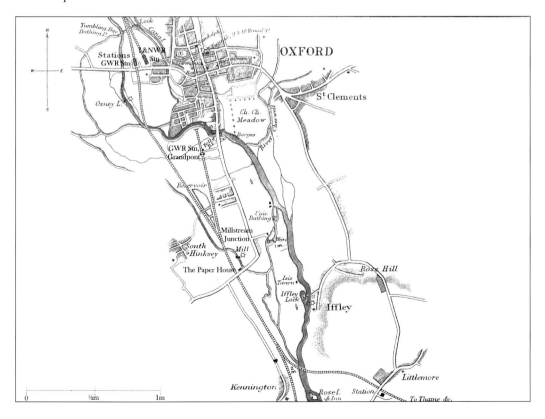

Taunt map dated 1879 showing the position of the 1844 and 1852 Great Western stations at Oxford. The map also shows Millstream Junction and the position of John Towle's paper house. (Courtesy Liz Woolley)

The 1852 Station

On 1 October 1852 the Birmingham and Oxford Junction line was duly opened through to Birmingham, and on the same date the new station at Botley Road was officially opened for passenger traffic; subsequently the old station at Grandpont was closed. However, due to its close proximity to the River Thames, for a number of years after closure it saw occasional use by excursion trains bringing visitors to nearby river events. The station, which had never been converted to standard gauge, continued in use as a goods depot until the broad gauge was removed from the area on 26 November 1872. The land not being required by the railway, it was sold for housing development and by 1880 all trace of the old station had disappeared, its site being covered by Marlborough Road.

The new station was constructed of timber and comprised a Brunel-designed overall roof that measured approximately 270ft in length and 125ft at its widest point. There were two main platforms; the up platform was 500ft in length with the down platform slightly longer at 594ft, with a 270ft long down bay at the north end. This bay was initially used by OW&WR standard gauge services, which from June 1853 had gained running rights into Oxford. A subway was provided, which ran from the City side of the station and under the whole station complex, thus giving foot passengers access to the down side platform without passing under the station bridge. Road access for cabs was provided on both up and down sides. Passenger waiting rooms were situated on each platform but for first- and second-class passengers only. Also on the up platform was a small refreshment room,

The only known image of the 1852 station showing the overall roof, taken here in 1875. The design is the same as was used at Banbury. The overall roof was removed when the station was rebuilt in 1890. The horse drawn cabs are standing on the entrance road. (Oxford History Centre)

A close up view of the steam pump house and water tower at Oxford taken in 1875. The water was pumped to the station area from the adjacent well. (Oxford History Centre)

which in 1867 is shown as under the management of Frank Williams. Initially, public toilets were provided on the up side only, but in 1864, with increasing complaints from the travelling public about accessibility and overcrowding, the staff-only toilets on the down side were opened up to the public. A separate goods platform and loading bay, accessed via a wagon turntable, was situated at the south end of the down platform. The new station was built at a slightly higher level than the surrounding area, with the line south of the station crossing the Botley Road via an overbridge. In order to provide adequate headroom, the road under the bridge was lowered, as can be clearly

seen to this day. This initially provided a 13ft headroom, but for over-sized loads a level crossing was provided just south of the road bridge.

Standing alongside the south end of the up platform was the station well and a steam pump house over which stood a 50,000 gallon water tank. The water from the well supplied the station area, and in the early years also the broad gauge engine shed.

Just to the south of the level crossing and on the down side stood a large three-road carriage shed. Constructed of wood with a slate roof it measured 174ft x 42ft; also adjacent to the carriage shed was a carpenter's shop and a smithy.

A view of the station bridge looking towards the City around the turn of the last century. On the right is the level crossing and the Great Western Station Hotel. On the left is the old turnpike house, which for many years traded as the 'Old Gatehouse' Pub. Currently it is operating as 'The One' restaurant and bar. (Author's Collection)

The steep entrance to the down side at Oxford. Notice the horse drawn cabs, lined up waiting for passengers. The cabs were all under the control of the Great Western Cab Inspector who allowed up to ten cabs daily to ply for trade on the down side. The horse drawn wagon on the left behind the cab belongs to B. Bennett, who for many years operated a Dry Cleaners and Dyers business from 15 Magdalen Street and his works at Abbey Place, St Ebbes. Just in view on the left is the shelter hut built for the cab drivers by the Great Western in 1907 and still *in situ* today. (Author's Collection)

The building was known locally as the West Midland carriage shed, being initially used by the West Midland Railway, and later the GWR, for the stabling and repair of carriage stock. The shed was probably constructed in around 1856, when mixed gauge lines were extended from Oxford to Reading and Paddington. This would have given the OW&WR (later West Midland Railway) standard gauge access to land south of the station. On 1 October 1861 standard gauge services were introduced between Paddington and Worcester via Oxford, but by this date the Great Western had essentially taken over the West Midland Railway services. Apart from the carriage shed the 1876 OS map also shows what is described as a coaling shed and water tank opposite the shed and in the up side Becket Street sidings;

this building measured approximately 31ft x 20ft. Interestingly the track diagram shows that it was only accessed from the south.

The first major alteration to the station was undertaken in November 1872 with the removal of the broad gauge. This now allowed the up and down platforms to be widened, the work being completed in August 1874. At this time the station area was controlled by two signal boxes, Oxford 'C', which was situated on the down side south of the Botley Road Bridge and alongside the level crossing, and at the north end by Oxford 'B', situated on the up side south of the river bridge. The removal of the old broad gauge engine shed in 1879 (which had been in use as a carriage shed) resulted in the provision of extra sidings at this point; these were

A view of the level crossing looking west in 1875 from Park End Street. On the left the small Oxford 'C' or Goods Shed signal box can be seen; it was replaced by a larger box in around 1908. Also on the left is the wooden office of Edwin J. Thomas, who operated as the West Midland Coal Stores. Just in view is the north edge of the West Midland Carriage shed. Notice also the wooden signal gantry fixed to the outside of the station bridge. (Oxford History Centre)

The Great Western ticket and enquiry office at 142 High Street pictured here in 1928, at this time the Great Western enquiry and receiving agent was Thomas Lloyd. To the right is No. 143, occupied by Wyatt and Sons (Carfax) Ltd, Drapers and Milliners. These buildings were situated at the south-east corner of Carfax. They were demolished in the 1930s and replaced with a modern stone structure. The GWR office was closed but Wyatt and Sons moved into the new building, which is currently occupied by the Edinburgh Woollen Mill. (Author's Collection)

reached via a new junction, which was constructed some 50 yards to the north. With the extra traffic being handled, together with many complaints from both the council and passengers alike, the Great Western decided to rebuild the station.

On 11 October 1890 the Great Western announced:

That the Directors of this Company have authorised the expenditure of nearly £10,000 for the purpose of providing better accommodation at Oxford Station, and that the contract for the greater part of it was let early

last month to Mr Samuel Robertson, contractor, Bristol, who is pushing on with the work with the greatest possible speed. The remainder of the work is being deferred, pending the settlement of the purchase of land required from the Corporation. The work in hand involves practically the remodelling of the passenger station. The large circular span roof with the square wooden columns is being taken away, and substituted by small iron columns in proportions of one to three of the present columns, and a small span roof (half glass) from the columns to the offices with a veranda and valance from the columns to and overlapping the edge of the platforms. The veranda and roof will be supported by lattice girders and brackets bolted to the columns. The up platform will be extended 115ft northward and the open platforms covered. Additional waiting rooms and a first-class lavatory will be built in the open spaces on the up and down platforms, and a new parcels and other offices at the south end of the up platform. The whole of the offices, including the booking office, will be rearranged and the latter thrown open to the platform. The subway is also to be improved and the shrubbery on the up side extended down to the Botley Road.

Although not mentioned it is probable that some degree of refurbishment and possibly enlargement of the refreshment room was undertaken at the same time.

The reference to the delay due to the purchase of land, referred to a narrow strip of land at Cripley Meadow.

This strip of land ran alongside the existing station and the adjacent houses and was required by the Company in order to lengthen the down platform and bay and provide two new sidings. The houses in Cripley Road and Abbey Road were constructed in 1878 by the Oxford builder John Dover, the roads being named around the same time. The council were asking £500 an acre for what the Great Western argued was essentially a useless piece of land at a price which they considered was too high. Eventually after a lot of negotiation the strip was sold to the railway at a greatly reduced price. The subsequent delay meant that work to extend both the up and down platforms and bays did not start until the autumn of 1907. At the same time the bridge over the Botley Road was widened to allow for a fourth track. On the down side the south end goods platform, sidings and wagon turntable were removed, the platform then being extended at the north and south to give a platform that was 907ft in length. At the same time the down departure bay was extended to 450ft. On the up side the platform was lengthened to 915ft, with the

Looking south from the down platform in the early 1900s. The line on the right foreground leads to a cattle dock and wagon turntable. Locos in view are a Queen Class 2-2-2, a Metropolitan 2-4-0T and an 0-6-0 Armstrong standard goods. On the far right is Oxford Goods signal box opened in 1873, being replaced by a new box in January 1908. (Author's Collection)

A view of the station from Station South signal box in the early 1930s. Notice the locomotive inspection pit at the end of the up platform. (Author's Collection)

up arrival bay also extended to 440ft. A major part of the work to accommodate the new bay connections resulted in the river bridge at the north end of the station being rebuilt and widened. In order to make room for the new down side bay connection, number four road at the engine shed was shortened at the river end by about 80ft. Other work undertaken at the same time saw scissors crossovers installed approximately half way along each platform line, thus connecting the platform lines to the up and down through lines. In 1910 the rebuilding work was completed when the previously uncovered section at the north end of the up platform was provided with a canopy roof for the majority of its length.

From the opening of the railway and right up until the present day there has been the provision of cabs to carry passengers to and from the station. In Oxford, as in many other towns and cities, the cabs were and still are subject to the local by-laws. Certainly during the nineteenth century the Great Western kept strict control over the horse-drawn cab operations at many of their stations.

In order to do this they would generally appoint a local Cab Inspector, as was the case at Oxford. Here it was the Cab Inspector's job to appoint and oversee the operation of the cabs and cab drivers using the station. It is not known if a Cab Inspector was employed by the Company at the old station at Grandpont as records do not exist. However it is probable that the Station Superintendent would have contracted with the various cab companies in the City to have cabs available for rail passengers. Luckily the Cab Inspector's report book for Oxford from 1869–1889 survives and gives a valuable insight into the Cab Inspector's duties. It states that contracts were renewed every three years, and stipulates that cabs, horses and drivers would be approved by appointed officers of the GWR, and could be removed or replaced if found unsatisfactory at any time. Cabs should be painted as required by the company, and plainly numbered and marked 'Great Western Railway, Oxford Station'. For the privilege of working at the station the cab proprietors were charged 2s/6d per week for each cab, payable on Monday mornings in advance. The Company were very strict on cab operations and the Inspector had the power to fine, suspend or even fire if necessary.

Misdemeanours and fines were clearly stated and included: drunkenness 10 shillings, insolence 5 shillings, overcharging 3 shillings, refusing to show (cabby) number, or not keeping place in rank 2s/6d, and for a breach of regulations for which a fine was not specified, 4 shillings (not quite sure what other misdemeanours this covered). These were not insignificant sums at the time. Persistent offenders could also be banned from operating at the station, which would mean no income at all for the specified time that they were banned, as cabs registered at the station could not ply for hire elsewhere in the City. Interestingly, City cabs were not under the control of the Great Western and could only set down at the station. The report book also shows the names of

the cab operators; under a new agreement dated Monday 11 June 1883 cabs would be supplied by just three proprietors, Mr Porter: 12 cabs, Mr Taylor: 7 cabs and Mr Higgs: 6 cabs, and that 'each proprietor will take up and down sides alternately two days at a time, the one whole turn is on the down side on Friday and Saturday, taking both sides on Sunday.' Importantly it states that 'each cabman as he returns from taking a fare will take his place at the bottom of the rank.' This etiquette is still operated by cab (taxi) drivers at Oxford station today. Another requirement that still exists is the payment of an annual registration fee to operate at the station. During these early years the cab drivers had no effective shelter from inclement weather, and it was not until in 1907 that the Great Western provided a cabman's shelter, adjacent to the down side station entrance. The building still survives and is currently in use as a café.

A view of Oxford looking north in around 1934. On the left are the West Midland carriage sidings; these were used for detached vans and coaches and also for the station south pilot locomotive. On the right is the Becket Street Yard which is full of general goods and coal wagons. (Author's Collection)

The down platform at Oxford taken in June 1935. The up and down platform cross overs can be seen to good effect. However with longer trains they saw little use other than for shunting purposes and were removed during the 1960s. (Author's Collection)

As far as I can ascertain the West Midland carriage shed was removed in around 1922. However, the sidings continued to be used for stabling coaches, the station south pilot locomotive, and in recent years DMUs and track machines. However, after some years out of use the two remaining West Midland sidings were removed in August 2017 during track renewal work at the south end of the station. Situated behind these sidings was the GWR, later Western Region, Staff Association club. This wooden building was probably opened on the site shortly after the removal of the West Midland carriage shed in around 1922 and stands almost exactly on the site of the carpenter's shop. At the time of writing the old building, although being closed for a number of years, is still *in situ*. Close inspection shows that it was almost certainly constructed from recycled timber. Which begs the question, did the timber for its construction come from the old West Midland carriage shed, or was the old wooden carpenter's shop converted into the club? As yet I have not found the answer.

Over the next 60 years the station saw little in the way of alteration or improvement, and by the 1950s had become very busy indeed. In 1953 the mid-week summer timetable lists 153 passenger trains, and 28 fish, parcels or empty stock trains. On Saturdays this number increased to 180 advertised passenger trains and 23 other, plus a number of Summer Saturday excursions. On top of this, at this time some 150 goods trains were passing through the station daily, with 120 of these calling or terminating at the various local yards. Over the years passenger numbers have grown; in 1958 in his article on Oxford, John Alves states that there were 620,000 passenger tickets issued, and 87,000 parcels forwarded and 320,000 received, and that at the beginning of each University term some 4,000 trunks and 800 bicycles passed through Oxford. I can well remember the down platform in particular being piled up with bicycles awaiting collection. How things have changed: in 2018 there are no parcels, no trunks and no bicycles. Students today mostly arrive by car and bring their bicycles with them.

The refreshment room on the up platform probably dates from the opening of the station in 1852; it was enlarged and refurbished during the station alterations in 1890. It is pictured here on 30 March 1948; notice also the 63½ milepost on the side of the platform face. (Author's Collection)

The up platform entrance and ticket collector's office remained almost unchanged right up to the demolition of the station in 1970. (Author's Collection)

Looking south from the down platform in 1953 shows the two wooden crossings at Oxford. In the foreground is the foot crossing for barrows and trolleys. Beyond it is the road crossing for vehicles that were too high to pass under the railway bridge. It was still in use at this date. A Southern King Arthur Class 4-6-0 waits for its train alongside the water tower in an area nicknamed locally as 'Mark's Hole'. (Author's Collection)

A station as busy as Oxford always required a large number of staff. In the 1930s the Great Western were employing around 1,300 in the various sections; even in 1958 some 1,111 male and female members of staff were being employed in the Oxford area. These comprised 360 in the operating department, 420 in the Locomotive Running and Maintenance department, with the remainder split between Goods, Commercial, Carriage and Wagon, Road Motor Engineers and Catering departments. During the last years of steam in the area there were still 144 loco crews working from Oxford. With the closure of so many departments, by 1985 staff numbers had reduced to just 209, a figure which included 51 drivers.

Today the station staff number around 80, with a further 86 train crew; these cover services to Paddington, Banbury, and the Cotswold line through to Hereford. The station shops and refreshment areas are nowadays privately run.

The up platform crossovers were removed in May 1966 and the down crossovers in May 1969. The main station buildings were essentially those that were constructed in 1852. By the 1960s much of the station was in a poor state of repair and the wooden structure was rotting in many places. For a number of years passengers, councillors and businesses had been regularly complaining about the appalling state of the structure and that 'British Rail should provide a station

A view of the approaches to the ex Great Western Station at Oxford taken in June 1958. On the right is the entrance to the ex LNWR goods depot. In the centre the main station entrance and entrance to the subway. On the left is the Botley Road railway bridge. (J.D. Edwards)

more in keeping with a University City.' Accordingly, during 1966 a proposal was made to construct a new and larger station at Oxford. With money at a premium at this time, to finance its construction the plans included a large amount of commercial development. This was strongly opposed locally and was eventually turned down by the Minister of Housing and Local Government. A second more modest proposal was made in 1969 but without any commercial development. They always say 'be careful what you wish for', and with no commercial development to help finance

its construction, in 1970 the old wooden station was demolished and replaced by a dreadful partially prefabricated flat roof structure that was obviously erected at the minimum of cost. The reconstruction work saw the subway closed and partially removed, and for the first time passengers travelling between the up and down platforms were able to use a new footbridge and lifts. At the same time the down bay and sidings were removed and replaced by a road to the now defunct diesel refuelling point. This was named Roger Dudman Way in 2002 and now provides access to a large development of

University post-graduate accommodation. On its completion in 1971 the new station was already being described as 'temporary', with a probable life span of about 10 years. However, with the gradual increase in passenger traffic, the station, and particularly the up side where the main entrance and exit was situated, was becoming increasingly congested. In 1985 a proposal was put forward to construct a new Parkway station on the site of the old up yard at Hinksey. The new station, Hinksey Parkway, would have had its own bus and car connection to the nearby Oxford Ring Road, which would have helped to alleviate the severe traffic congestion at the main station in Oxford. Like all new ideas there were considerable local objections, not just from local inhabitants but surprisingly also from many local councillors, which resulted in Hinksey Parkway being

abandoned. Interestingly a prefabricated station structure had previously been constructed in anticipation, but with the project abandoned it was taken to Devon where it became Tiverton Parkway.

With Hinksey Parkway abandoned, in 1989 a decision was made to improve the station, and in 1990 the up side buildings were removed and replaced by a large brick structure with a gabled roof. The much improved building now houses numerous shops, toilets and an enlarged ticket office. On the down side the café and toilets were refurbished, and apart from some minor modifications the 1971 'temporary' flat roofed platform awnings on platforms 3 and 4 remain pretty much intact. For many years the station had a small but busy travel centre. Opened in 1975 it was situated on the up side and in 1985 the staff of five were dealing with around 400,000 enquires

The up platform at Oxford pictured here around 1900. The station bookstall see here on the right was at this time operated by W H Smith. This company lost its contract with the Great Western in 1905, due to a rent dispute. During the same year a new contract was awarded to its rival Wyman & Sons. Wyman's operated at Oxford until 1959 when the Company was taken over by John Menzies who operated the newsagents and bookstall until the old station was demolished in 1970. John Menzies was acquired by W H Smith in 1998, who once again operate the newsagents at Oxford. (Great Western Trust)

a year. It was closed in 1990, and today enquires are now dealt with by the ticket office staff, but increasingly the public are using the internet for their travel information. In December 2016 the new Chiltern Railways route from Marylebone was opened through to Oxford. The old up bay and adjacent sidings were rebuilt to provide two new platforms for these services, being numbered platforms 1 and 2. As part of the work the 1910 station canopy at the north end of the up platform was removed and replaced by a new and larger canopy. The opening of the new Chiltern platforms saw the old Great Western platforms numbered 3 and 4. In July 2018 the down platform was converted to multi directional running, and at the same time the up platform has been raised and completely resurfaced. Interestingly, even today on the down side one can clearly see remaining parts of the brickwork of the 1852 platform. Another

welcome addition is the opening of a new ticket gate adjacent to platforms 1 and 2 and this has greatly eased the congestion problem at the existing ticket gate on platform 3. At the north end of platform 1 a new prefabricated accommodation building has been constructed. This contains facilities for train crews, guards and on-train catering staff. Storage facilities have also been provided for the various station retail units and also Rail Gourmet for the preparation of food and drinks for its on-train catering service.

In July 2018 extensive work was carried out at Oxford by Network Rail to bring the signalling up to date and to convert the down side platform to bi-directional running. At the same time the small signalling cabin on the down side was closed, with signalling in the area being taken over by the Thames Valley Signalling Centre at Didcot. The track layout through the station has

The up side of the 1970 station at Oxford on 26 May 1978. This was a poor replacement of the old 1852 station. It did not last for long and was replaced by the current station in 1990. However, the down platform currently still retains much of the 1970s structure. (Author's Collection)

been improved to allow for higher train speeds. North of the station, the down loop between Oxford and Wolvercote that was opened on 3 March 1942 and was closed in 1973 has now been reinstated and is used by both freight and Cotswold line passenger traffic. In recent years considerable work has been undertaken upgrading the Cotswold line to provide a double-track railway between Evesham and Charlbury. However, for monetary reasons a passing loop was never installed over the 10 mile single-track section between Charlbury and Wolvercote Junction. An omission that regularly results in late running.

The growth in passenger numbers has seen the need for a new larger station again on the agenda. In 2017/18 some 7,984,000 journeys were made, quite a staggering increase compared to the 1958 total of just 650,000. At the time of writing there is talk of rebuilding the station once again. One suggestion is to widen the Botley Road Bridge and demolish the Youth Hostel building. The down platform would then become an island platform thus increasing capacity at peak times. At the same time the current station administrative offices would move to the down side.

Although a considerable amount of preparation work was undertaken for the electrification of the Oxford branch, at the time of writing Oxford appears to have been forgotten, and electrification is probably still years away.

The following list is of Stationmasters known to have served at Oxford; these have been obtained from various Oxford Trade Directories published between 1844 and 1962.

A survivor from the early days of the railway is the now closed Great Western/Western Region staff club, pictured here on 5 January 2019. The building stands on the site of the old West Midland carpenters' shop south of the station. It was probably opened in the early 1920s and it appears to have been constructed from reclaimed timber, possibly from the demolished West Midland Carriage shed. (Author)

The station entrance hall at Oxford, nowadays a very busy place. In 2017/18 the annual passenger usage at Oxford was just under 8 million, due in no small measure to the opening of the Chiltern Railways route to Marylebone. (This figure is the annual estimated passenger usage based upon ticket sales.) (Author)

Frederick (Frank) Price was the Oxford Stationmaster from 1941 until 1951. In 1947 the Company purchased a motorcycle to enable him to cover his area. This cartoon drawn by the Oxford Artist Alan Course appeared in both the *Oxford Mail* and the *Great Western Magazine*. (Author's Collection)

The Queen being introduced to James (Jim) Miller, the Oxford Stationmaster, on her visit to Oxford on 4 November 1960. Jim Miller was well regarded locally and was the Stationmaster at Oxford from 1951 until his retirement in 1962. (Author's Collection)

Great Western Stationmasters

First station at Grandpont opened in June 1844

James Kelley is shown as Station Inspector/Superintendent 1844–1854

It is probable that after the closure of Grandpont James Kelley became the station superintendent at the new station at Park End Street.

James F. Relton, 1854–1863
Alfred Jorden, 1863–1866

William Miles Beauchamp, 1866–1868
James William Gibbs, 1868–1880
Albert Newsom, 1880–1883
Robert Davis, 1883–1905
Richard Brooker, 1905–1918
William Frederick Knutton, 1918–1924
Alfred Charles Foster, 1924–1927
Francis Herbert Buckingham (Frank), April 1927–October 1941 (from 1933 the GWR stationmaster was also the Stationmaster at Rewley Road)
Frederick Charles Price, 1941–1951

The upside ticket office in 1963, with the ticket racks full of Edmondson tickets. In the centre is Len Adams and on the right David Green. (Author's Collection)

James Miller (Jim), 1951–1962
Charles W. Swancott, 1962–1964

James Miller was the last true Stationmaster at Oxford. After his retirement in 1962 the station was placed under the control of a station manager.

The Great Western never constructed a Stationmaster's house at Oxford, with all Stationmasters residing in private properties in the City, which one assumes were provided by the GWR. Both Frederick Price and his successor Jim Miller resided at 74 Abingdon Road.

Chapter 4

THE BRANCH LINES

The Abingdon Railway

Of the four local branch lines the
Abingdon Railway was the oldest.
The first mention of a branch line to
Abingdon, the County town of Berkshire,
was made in 1837 as part of the proposal
for the Oxford Railway. The 1837 Oxford
Bill failed and subsequent proposals
for an Oxford Railway including the
successful Act of 11 April 1843 did
not include a branch to Abingdon.
This was in no small part due to
objections from Thomas Duffield, the
Member of Parliament for Abingdon
from 1832 until 1844, as well as from a
number of councillors. The idea of an
Abingdon branch was not revived until
a new proposal was put forward by the
Abingdon Railway Company in January
1855. This time it was successful and on
20 June 1855 Royal Assent was given for
a 1¾ mile long broad gauge branch to
Abingdon. The line was constructed in
less than a year and opened for traffic
on Monday 2 June 1856. The newly
completed line was inspected on 15 May
by Captain Galton who reported:

> I have inspected the Abingdon
> Railway, which is a short branch
> railway 1 mile 55 chains in length
> from its Junction with the Oxford
> and Didcot line to Abingdon. The
> line runs nearly along the surface of

the country and there are no bridges
either under or over nor is it crossed
by any public roads.

He goes on to report:

> The main platforms now are
> complete. There are no turntables
> on the line. The system under which
> traffic is to be conducted is that the
> engine will be maintained on the line
> to work all trains. Company have
> undertaken that only one engine in
> steam shall be allowed on the line at
> one and the same time and that this
> engine shall be a tank engine.

The branch connected with the Oxford
to Didcot line via a pair of interchange
platforms which were situated at milepost
57¾ and approximately a quarter of a mile
north of the Thames bridge at Nuneham.
The interchange station was shown on
the map as 'Abingdon Junction' but
never appeared in the public timetables.
It was quite a basic structure: its wooden
platforms contained a small wooden
waiting room on the up side while there
was also a run-round loop for the branch
train. Interestingly, the platforms were
only accessible by rail, and were solely
used for changing trains. There was no
footbridge and passengers travelling on
up services were required to cross the
main line on the level.

Class 850 0-6-0PT No. 1976 with the branch set of four-wheeled coaches stands at Radley in around 1930 with the service to Abingdon. The four-wheeled coaches were removed from the branch services during 1931, when auto-coach working was introduced. No. 1976 was built as a saddle tank in September 1890, converted to a pannier tank in September 1929 and withdrawn in November 1936. It was allocated to Oxford from May 1927 until November 1932. (Author's Collection)

A shot of Radley in 1925. In the foreground is the roof of the small building that was removed from Abingdon Junction and was used for many years at Radley as a goods office. Domestic coal is being unloaded by hand onto a 'Radley Stores' lorry for delivery locally. At this time Radley Stores was owned by one Samuel Harry Gould. (Author's Collection)

The construction of the branch was accomplished with few difficulties, passing over flat ground to terminate in Abingdon adjacent to Stert Street. In order to accommodate the terminus seven properties including the well known Plough Inn were purchased by the company, the rest of the land being purchased from the Borough of Abingdon. The terminus station comprised a single platform that was partially covered by an overall roof, with a small timber and brick booking office at the town end. A small goods yard was provided, together with a stable for the delivery horses that were used by the railway. A single-road engine shed stood at the east end of the yard, constructed of stone with a slated timber roof and timber ends. A wooden coal stage and watering facility were also provided. From the start the branch was operated using Great Western locomotives and rolling stock. However the Abingdon Railway

Company continued as an independent company until 15 August 1904 after which it was absorbed by the Great Western. Shareholders received £20 of Great Western ordinary stock for every £10 Abingdon Railway share.

As per the 1856 Inspector's report the branch was operated on a one engine in steam principle with branch trains running to and from the interchange platform where they connected with Oxford branch stopping services.

The broad gauge was removed from Abingdon between 25 and 27 November 1872; after its removal the branch was extended northwards for approximately ¾ mile to a new station at Radley. On 8 September 1873 the old interchange platforms were closed, with Abingdon branch services now running to and from Radley. The new station contained two main line platforms; the Abingdon branch platform was situated on the down side thus forming an island platform.

The original station at Abingdon around the turn of the last century. Standing outside are some of the station staff together with a small horse-drawn wagon. (Author's Collection)

Another early picture shows some of the yard staff, together with the signalman and the driver and fireman of 850 Class 0-6-0ST No. 2017 at Abingdon in around 1899. No. 2017 was built in February 1895, converted to a pannier tank in June 1922, and withdrawn in March 1951. (Great Western Trust)

A small signal box, which controlled the branch and exchange sidings, was constructed at the south end of the down platform. This was replaced in December 1895 by a new 41 lever signal box that was constructed on the south end of the up platform. Passengers initially crossed the line via a level crossing at the north end of the station, but in 1883 a footbridge was constructed connecting the down island platform to the up side station entrance and booking hall. Interestingly the wooden waiting room from the interchange station was moved to Radley and saw use for many years as a platelayers' hut.

The June 1876 timetable shows 15 passenger services in each direction on weekdays, three of which were mixed trains. The Sunday service comprised five trains in each direction.

On 22 April 1908, shortly before 7am, a 17-wagon goods train being shunted by a 517 Class 0-4-2T failed to stop due to a lack of adhesion on the wet track, and collided with the four coach 7.05am branch service that was standing in the platform. The weight of the goods train pushed the coaches forward with the rear two being shunted up over the stop blocks and into the station building, causing severe damage to both the building and the overall roof. The 50-year-old building which was already in a poor state of repair was subsequently demolished and replaced with a more substantial structure. This was constructed during 1909/10 in English Bond brickwork with a slate roof

On 22 April 1908 a goods train being shunted in the yard collided with the empty branch passenger coaches standing in the station. The resultant damage to the station fabric saw it demolished and replaced by a new building. (Author's Collection)

The newly constructed station building in 1910. Notice the amount of advertising on view. (Author's Collection)

and a rather splendid round pediment containing the station name. At the same time the remains of the wooden train shed were removed and replaced by a new platform canopy.

The branch continued to operate without any major incidents. The 1922 timetable shows 16 services on weekdays in each direction with five on Sundays, one of which ran to and from Oxford. The weekday service included three mixed trains, and two separate goods only trains. The introduction of auto train working on the branch during 1931 saw an increase in weekday services to 18 each way, with some extra trains on Saturday evenings. Three of the services were mixed, and there were two daily goods services. With its close proximity to the River Thames, the Great Western and later Western Region, in co-operation with Salter's Steamers, operated special combined rail/river trips to and from Oxford. One could travel from Paddington to Oxford by train, have a tour of the colleges and then on the Thames to

Abingdon, before returning by train to Paddington.

The branch saw extra freight and passenger traffic when in 1929 the MG Car Company moved from its cramped base at Edmund Road in Cowley to Abingdon into part, and later all, of the old Pavlova Leather Factory site. The success of the MG brand worldwide and the ability to move them by rail meant that over the years many thousands of Abingdon-built cars were shipped out for export from the railhead at Abingdon to the docks at Grimsby, Newport and Southampton.

By the 1950s the weekday passenger service comprised 11 trains in each direction with four extra on Saturdays. Sunday services comprised just three up and four down trains. On weekdays there were two morning and one afternoon goods services that ran to and from Hinksey yard. During this period the town saw little expansion, and as with many other branch lines, the increasing use of private cars meant that passenger numbers were never at a level to sustain

The terminus in the early 1920s. Notice the unusually wide platform. In later years the Oxford to Abingdon buses terminated here. (Author's Collection)

A view of the station area in 1958. The signal box was opened around 1885 and housed a 20 lever frame. By this date it had closed and been replaced by a ground frame which can just be seen at the front of the box. (Author's Collection)

the railway. The introduction of a single car DMU in the early 1960s did little to increase passenger numbers or improve running costs. It was no surprise when the branch was closed to passenger services on 9 September 1963.

The small goods yard remained open for coal and MG car traffic, with services to and from Hinksey being operated using Class 08, 22 and 31 diesels. In 1971 the attractive station building was demolished and regular goods services effectively ceased with the closure of the MG car plant on 24 October 1980. With the car traffic gone the only customer left was the local Charrington's coal yard, which was served as required with a Class 08 shunter working the local trip from Hinksey. The last inwards coal train operated on

27 March 1984, after which date the yard and branch were closed. British Rail ran their customary special passenger train using three-car DMU No. L585 on 30 June 1984. There was some talk at this time of the Great Western Society operating the branch as a heritage railway but this came to nothing. In June 1986 work started on removing the track, and some 130 years after it opened the Abingdon branch was no more. For a number of years after closure the station area remained derelict, with part of the yard being used as a car park. However, on 22 March 1994 a new Waitrose food store was opened on the site of the old station, and since then the rest of the station area has been extensively redeveloped and is now covered by a care home, flats, houses, and a large car park.

The station pictured in 1959. Today this area is covered with a supermarket and car park. (Author's Collection)

Motive Power

Broad Gauge

The 1856 Gooch engine records show that Sharpe Roberts Co 2-2-2 *Eagle*, built in November 1838, was at Abingdon to work the first trains. Also listed at Abingdon at this time was 2-2-2 back tank *Aeolus*. In December 1856 this had been replaced by Leo Class 2-4-0ST *Etna*. Both locomotives are shown as still at work at Abingdon in 1857 and 1858, but in May 1859 *Eagle* is shown as working at Henley, being replaced at Abingdon by 2-2-2 back tank *Vulcan*. This engine was built by Charles Tayleur and Co in November 1837. Other locomotives listed as working from Abingdon during this period are Leo Class 2-4-0ST *Hecla* and another Sharp Roberts Co 2-2-2ST *Atlas*. Broad gauge records after this date are missing but *Atlas*, which was withdrawn in June 1872, may have been one of the last broad gauge locomotives to work on the branch.

Standard Gauge

Standard gauge days saw a succession of small tank locomotives being used on Abingdon branch services, with the 517 Class 0-4-2Ts being the usual motive power from 1872 right through to 1947. One of the 517s, No. 1473 *Fair Rosamund*, the regular locomotive on the Woodstock branch, was allocated to Abingdon between September and December 1907. Other types noted as working at Abingdon were Class 850 and 2021 0-6-0 tanks, and between 2 March 1900 and 10 August 1901 the ex-Monmouthshire Railway & Canal Company 4-4-0T No. 1306 was allocated to Oxford for general work, which included use for a short time on Abingdon branch services. In 1931 the branch service changed forever with the withdrawal of the old four-wheeled coaching stock and the introduction of single-class auto-car working. These services were initially worked by auto-fitted 517 Class 0-4-2Ts. One of these, No. 1159, built in 1876, was allocated to Oxford in October 1934 and for the next ten years worked many of the branch services. It was still being used on the Abingdon to Hinksey freights right up until its withdrawal from Oxford in August 1947. It was the last surviving member of the 517 Class. From July 1935 the motive power changed when auto- fitted 4800 Class 0-4-2Ts Nos. 4843 and 4850 were allocated to Oxford. During this period the branch locomotive was still being serviced at Abingdon until the ex-broad gauge engine shed was officially closed on 20 March 1954. After this date the branch loco was serviced at Oxford, from where it would run down light engine each morning to work the branch, returning to Oxford for servicing each evening. During the final years services over the branch were operated using at various times 4800 Class 0-4-2T Nos. 1420/35/42/44/47/48/50. From 1962 and until closure to passengers on 9 September 1963, services were operated using a single car Class 121 DMU. The last

official steam hauled passenger train ran on 23 July 1963 when Abingdon School ran an excursion to Coventry. The seven coach train was hauled over the branch by 0-6-0PT No. 1627, and after picking up four more coaches at Radley, which included ex-Great Western 12-wheeled buffet car No. W9677W, the 11-coach train was hauled as far as Leamington by Hall Class 4-6-0 No. 6983 *Otterington Hall*. It was reported that on its return the whole train ran back along the branch to Abingdon, again hauled by No. 1627. The 5700 Class 0-6-0PTs had been allowed on the branch during September 1963 and were used to operate many of the freight services. As already mentioned, after the demise of steam on the branch in December 1965 freight services were hauled using Class 08 and Class 22 diesels, the former being used until closure in March 1984. Interestingly, of the 4800 Class 0-4-2Ts used during the final years, Nos. 1420, 1442 and 1450 all survive in preservation.

An unidentified 4300 class 2-6-0 on an up class D express freight speeds through Radley in June 1963. The signal box was closed on 25 May 1965 and replaced by a ground frame which was situated on the down side to the east of the branch platform. (D. Tuck)

Ex-Great Western 4800 class 0-4-2T No. 1444 waits to depart from Radley with the auto-coach service to Abingdon on 16 November 1959. (A. E. Doyle)

No. 1444 shortly after arriving at Abingdon on 16 November 1959. (A. E. Doyle)

No. 1435 takes water as it prepares to depart with the 4pm goods service to Hinksey on 7 September 1961. (A. E. Doyle)

The rundown terminus at Abingdon on 10 May 1962. The Great Western seat has seen better days and the old gas lamp on the right has been converted to electric. The Western Region delivery vehicle is an Austin FG / S200/404, a type introduced in 1960. (C. G. Stuart)

The 9.50am service to Radley formed by Pressed Steel Motor brake second No. W55031 at Abingdon on 19 May 1962. The single car DMUs had taken over Abingdon branch services during 1961 but with low passenger numbers the branch was closed to passengers on 9 September 1963. (C. G. Stuart)

The 4pm Abingdon to Hinksey goods hauled by 0-4-2T No. 1450 stands in the branch platform at Radley in May 1962. (A. E. Doyle)

MGB and MG Midget sports cars as far as the eye can see in September 1974. The MGs were generally shipped from Abingdon to either Grimsby or Newport Docks, however the photographer remembers that these were bound for Southampton. The train is in two sections due to lack of siding space but will be joined together for its journey to the docks. (Laurence Johnston)

The Witney Railway

During the nineteenth century Witney was an important centre for the wool trade and blanket making. As with many other small towns it suffered from poor road links which affected the expansion of local trade. As early as 1836 there was a proposal by the London and Birmingham Railway to construct a line from Tring to Cheltenham, running via Thame, Witney and Burford, but this scheme was rejected by Parliament. In 1845 another similar proposal by the London & North Western Railway was also rejected. On 23 December 1858 a number of local tradesmen called a public meeting to discuss the possibility of constructing a Witney Railway, and with much local support the Witney Railway Company was formed. It was envisaged that the

proposed line would connect with the Oxford Worcester & Wolverhampton Railway's route into Oxford via a junction at Yarnton. Initially the Great Western opposed the plan, but on 1 August 1859 a bill for an eight mile single-line standard gauge branch from Yarnton to Witney was given Royal Assent. The construction of the railway was let to the contractor Joseph Pickering, and work started at Eynsham on 19 May 1860.

Two days before the start of work, on 17 May 1860 the Witney Railway Company had entered into an agreement with the OW&WR that it should work the branch for a period of 10 years in exchange for 50 per cent of the gross receipts. Less than one month later the OW&WR became part of the West Midland Railway, who took over the agreement to work the branch. With little major engineering work

A service to Witney and Fairford waits to depart from the down bay platform at Oxford, hauled by GWR Metropolitan Class 2-4-0T No. 3585 in around 1934. (Great Western Trust)

The Metro 2-4-0s had a long association with the branch. Here No. 3562 stands at Eynsham on 25 September 1948 with a five coach service to Witney and Fairford. The crossing loop and concrete platform were installed during August 1944. No. 3562 was built in February 1894 and withdrawn from Oxford in March 1949. (M. Yarwood)

being required, work progressed quickly and with construction in an advanced state, on 10 August 1861 a special train traversed the length of the branch in order to allow the Directors to inspect their new railway. The line left the West Midland Railway's Oxford to Worcester line via a junction at Yarnton, and ran via Cassington and Eynsham to a small one platform station on the east of Witney. On Wednesday 13 November 1861 and to great jubilation in the town, which had declared a public holiday for the occasion, the branch was officially opened. The local newspaper reported the station had been decorated for the occasion and that the first train arrived at 2pm. Later that day the Directors and their guests adjourned to the nearby Marlborough Hotel for a celebration dinner.

On Thursday 14 November 1861 the branch was opened to the general public, intermediate stations being provided at South Leigh, Eynsham and Yarnton.

Passenger traffic comprised four trains in each direction between Witney and Oxford with a journey time of just 35 minutes. These departed from Witney at 8.15am, 11.00am, 4.50pm and 7.35pm, and from Oxford at 9.00am, 11.50am, 5.40pm and 8.30pm. The return fares were set at 2s 6d first-class, 1s 9d second-class and 1s 3d third-class. These early services were probably worked by West Midland locomotives. A small single-road engine shed was provided at Witney where the branch locomotives were serviced. However goods services over the branch were delayed until 1 March 1862 due apparently to a dispute regarding unfinished work by the contractor Joseph Pickering. The remaining work was taken over and eventually finished by Malachi Barnett, a local contractor. It seems rather ironic that after absorbing the West Midland Railway on 1 August 1863, the Great Western, which had in 1859 objected to the construction of the branch, should

The branch left the main line to Worcester at Yarnton Junction, pictured here in 1959 looking towards Oxford. The signal box was opened on 13 June 1909 and replaced two earlier boxes; it stood 14ft above rail level so that the signalman could have a clear view of both junctions. One of these, the Yarnton Loop to Banbury Road Junction, can be seen on the left. The signal box was closed on 29 March 1971. (Michael Hale)

The 12.15pm service from Oxford to Fairford hauled by 2251 Class 0-6-0 No. 2294 takes the Fairford branch at Yarnton Junction in 1958. (Author's Collection)

take over its operation and provide both the motive power and coaching stock.

The impact of the opening on travel times is related in a light hearted article that appeared in *Jackson's Oxford Journal* of 16 November 1861:

> He (Mr C. Clinch) remembered his grandfather telling him what a serious affair a journey from Witney to London was in his day – that the manufacturers put their affairs in order, and made their wills, doubting whether they should ever return – they then confined themselves to a lumbering stage coach, and to the tender mercies of a Jehu who had a propensity to pull up at almost every alehouse on the road, and at length reached their destination, after travelling a night and a day. Under the new state of things an inhabitant of Witney might take his breakfast with his family, get to London in two and a half hours, spend a long day there and return home to a late dinner.

The East Gloucestershire Railway had been formed at a meeting at Cheltenham on 25 October 1861 to construct a second and shorter route to London that would run between Cheltenham and Faringdon (Oxon) via Fairford and Lechlade; at Faringdon it would then connect with the Great Western Paddington to Bristol main Line. A connecting link from Lechlade to Witney was also in the proposal, and this would have put Witney on a direct route from London to Cheltenham. However, as with many early schemes, the whole project was under-financed, which resulted in the Cheltenham to Faringdon section being abandoned. The East Gloucestershire Company now concentrated on extending the existing Witney Railway for 14 miles and 10 chains to the Gloucestershire market town of Fairford, with the proviso that should finances improve it would finish the line from there to Cheltenham. Royal Assent for this section was obtained on 29 July 1864 to construct a single line between Cheltenham and Oxford via Charlton

Kings, Fairford, Lechlade and Witney, where it would connect with the existing Witney Railway. There were no major engineering works required, but the construction was still delayed by lack of finances. However, on 10 January 1873 the line was finally finished between Witney and Fairford, being opened for inspection on the same day. On 14 January the customary celebration opening took place, with a Great Western 517 Class 0-4-2ST hauling a nine coach train from Oxford through to Fairford. The line opened for passenger services the following day, 15 January. The new extended branch was worked from the start by the Great Western, who, as with the Witney Railway had agreed to operate the branch for 10 years for a return of 50 per cent of gross receipts. The early East Gloucester Railway timetables comprise four passenger trains a day in each direction, two of which were mixed. The journey time for the 25½ miles was around 70 minutes, with return fares to Oxford set at 5s 6d first-class, 3s 9d second-class and 1s 3d third-class. The working timetable for this period also shows a Sunday cattle train in each direction, comprising the 2.00pm down empties from Oxford and the 3.20pm up ex-Fairford loaded.

This new line resulted in the construction of a new station at Witney, which was situated on the extension line; a new goods junction connected the old and new lines. The original terminus station at Witney was then closed to passengers, becoming the town's goods station. Passing points on the new extension were initially provided at Witney and at Bampton but with the increase in wartime traffic on the branch two other passing points were opened, at Eynsham on 6 August 1944, and at Carterton on 2 October 1944.

The East Gloucester Railway remained an independent company until 1890 when the whole of the branch from Yarnton Junction to Fairford was taken over by the Great Western Railway. The original proposal to extend the line from Fairford

Eynsham Sugar Beet and Crop Dryers Ltd opened a small factory at Eynsham in 1927. It is pictured here, probably soon after opening. The factory was short-lived and closed in 1931. During the Second World War the sidings were extended and the site used by the Royal Army Service Corps. (Author's Collection)

5700 class 0-6-0PT No. 9640 stands in the goods yard at Witney in May 1959. This was the site of the original Witney Railway station. (Michael Hale)

to Cheltenham was soon abandoned by the Great Western. Had the line been built in its entirety, it would have certainly been an important through route. The subsequent abandonment resulted in the branch effectively ending at a pair of buffer stops about a quarter of a mile west of Fairford station, which itself was situated some three quarters of a mile from the town. A small single-road engine shed constructed of wood, together with a turntable, watering and coaling facilities were provided to service the locomotives working the branch services; these were supplied by the main depot at Oxford. The opening of the sub-shed at Fairford in January 1873 resulted in the closure of the locomotive shed at Witney.

In the early 1900s the Great Western was experimenting with its Automatic Train Control System (ATC) and in 1906, as an experiment, the system was installed on the Witney Branch. It was the first time it had been used on a single line and it proved to be so successful that every distant signal between Fairford and the junction at Yarnton was removed and replaced with an ATC ramp. As a result only locomotives fitted with ATC apparatus were allowed to work over the branch. The branch was controlled by

eight signal boxes; these were situated at Yarnton Witney Junction, and on the branch itself at Eynsham (19 levers), Witney Goods Junction (13 levers), Witney (19 levers), Bampton (19 levers), Carterton (18 levers), Lechlade (17 levers) and Fairford (13 levers). In 1883 there were two separate boxes that controlled the junctions at Yarnton. The first of these, Yarnton Witney Junction, controlled the Witney branch junction, the second, Yarnton Oxford Road Junction, controlled the junction between the OW&WR and the LNWR loop line to Banbury Road Junction. Both boxes were closed on 13 June 1909 and replaced by a new and larger 50 lever frame Yarnton Junction Signal Box. During the Second World War on 8 August 1944 a new 18 lever box was opened at Carterton. With the closure of the Fairford branch to passenger traffic all signal boxes on the line were closed during July and August 1962. However, the large box at Yarnton Junction remained open, and was not closed until 28 March 1971.

The idea of a shorter route to Cheltenham was still very much in the minds of local businessmen and councillors. In October 1923 a proposal was put to the Great Western 'for the building of a new line some eight miles in length

Witney Station Signal Box taken here in May 1959. It was opened in 1893 and contained a 19 lever frame. It was closed on 11 July 1962. (Author's Collection)

Metro 2-4-0T No. 3588 at the Fairford terminus with a service to Oxford in the 1930s. (Author's Collection)

from Fairford to Cirencester at an estimated cost of £321,000'. This would connect with the Midland & South Western Junction Railway at Cirencester and provide a new shorter route to Cheltenham. The Great Western unfortunately did not support the proposal, pointing out that shortening the route would lead to a general loss of revenue elsewhere, and the extra employment it would bring locally would be negligible. They therefore concluded that the extra traffic would not justify the cost of construction. The government of the day accepted the Great Western's objection and the proposal was abandoned.

By the early 1900s services on the branch comprised five passenger trains daily between Oxford and Fairford and a return Thursdays-only service from Oxford to Witney. There was just one return service on Sundays. The 1928 timetable had the addition of two services to Witney and two additional services on Saturdays only, again there was just one afternoon service on Sunday with a return service in the evening. The extended section between Witney

and Fairford never really produced the expected revenue, and it was only during the Second World War with the opening of airfields at Carterton (Brize Norton) and Fairford that passenger usage increased. With the sudden influx of military personnel using the branch a new station with up and down platforms was opened at Carterton on 2 October 1944. Bampton, which was also adjacent to the new airfield, was renamed Brize Norton and Bampton on 1 May 1940.

After the war the service settled down to six in each direction between Oxford and Fairford, with two services on Sunday. There was also one down and two up weekday services between Carterton and Oxford. By 1960 the increasing use of cars and buses resulted in a reduction in passengers using the branch. Subsequently services were reduced to four in each direction on weekdays plus an early morning up service from Carterton to Oxford; there was no Sunday service.

In 1927 a sugar beet factory was opened at Eynsham by Sugar Beet and Crop Dryers Ltd. The factory was served by three

Ex-Great Western 5700 class 0-6-0PT No. 9654 stands in the up bay at Oxford on 23 May 1962 after arriving with the 1.55pm service from Fairford. The branch closed to passengers the following month. (Author's Collection)

BRITISH TRANSPORT COMMISSION
BRITISH RAILWAYS (WESTERN REGION)

PUBLIC NOTICE

The British Transport Commission hereby give notice that on and from Monday, 18th June, 1962, the passenger train service between Oxford and Fairford together with stops at Yarnton in the Oxford/Worcester Line services will be permanently withdrawn, and the line between Witney (exclusive) and Fairford will be closed for all purposes. The parcels facilities at Eynsham and South Leigh will also be withdrawn.

The City of Oxford Motor Services Limited, who already operate passenger road services between Oxford and Lechlade, will provide additional services between Witney and Fairford affording connections with existing services at Witney from and to Oxford; details can be obtained on application to the Omnibus Company.

Arrangements for the collection and delivery of parcels traffic, small consignments of freight traffic and other freight traffic now normally carted by the Commission in the area will be maintained. Facilities for the handing in and/or collection of parcels and freight traffic will be retained at Witney and similar facilities are available at Oxford, Faringdon and Cirencester Town stations.

Facilities for dealing with freight traffic in full truck loads will be retained at Witney, South Leigh and Eynsham and similar facilities are available at Oxford, Faringdon and Cirencester Town Stations.

Any further information required can be obtained on application to :—

Mr. G. A. V. PHILLIPS,

Divisional Manager, Paddington Station, London, W.2.
(Telephone : Paddington 7000, Ext. 2304) or

THE STATION MASTER

at Oxford (Tel: Oxford 49551), Witney (Tel. Witney 4), Faringdon (Tel. Faringdon 3152) or Cirencester Town (Tel. Cirencester 782) stations

Closure notice for the branch passenger services from Monday 18 June 1962. (Author's Collection)

sidings and generated extra goods traffic on the branch. Interestingly the works operated its own locomotive, ex-Great Western 0-4-0ST No. 921 built in 1906 and which was used for shunting the sidings. The sugar beet plant closed in 1931, the locomotive being sold in December of the same year to a private company in Kent. In 1940 the site was taken over by the Royal Army Service Corps and at the same time the sidings were enlarged to provide five through roads. After the war the site was used for a time by the Colonial Development Corporation as a storage depot, but in 1956 it lost its rail connection when the one remaining siding was closed. For many years the goods traffic over the branch comprised a twice-daily goods service from Oxford to Fairford. But by the 1950s only the early morning service was running through to Fairford, with the other now terminating at Witney. Witney was the only really busy station on the branch, and figures for 1957 show that 44,000 tons of goods and 66,000 parcels were handled at the station. It was only this volume of traffic that sustained the branch during its final years of operation. The increase in road haulage, together with the steady decline of the Witney blanket industry, meant that passengers alone could not justify the losses being incurred, and it was no surprise when the line was closed to passengers on 18 June 1962. However the original Witney (old station) to Yarnton section remained open for freight traffic, serving mainly a coal yard operated by Marriotts, the local coal merchant. In later years the twice weekly freight was operated using the rather unsuccessful North British Type 2 (Class 22) locomotives. In 1970 it was revealed that the cost of maintaining the branch considerably outstripped the receipts, and on 2 November 1970 the remaining section of the Witney branch was closed completely. Prior to closure, on 31 October 1970 a British Rail sponsored nine car DMU, *Witney Wanderer*, became the last passenger train to traverse the

branch. I was a passenger on that train and can remember having to wait whilst the crossing gate at South Leigh was opened manually by the crew.

Periodically there have been calls to re-open the branch to Witney. On 17 January 2019 the Witney Oxford Transport Group proposed a new branch that would run from Handborough on the Cotswold line through to Carterton, via Eynsham, Ducklington and Witney, with a cost estimate of £285 million. It is unlikely that this will get off the ground, as a major upgrade of the heavily congested A40 trunk road between Oxford and Witney has already been agreed at a cost of £180 million.

Motive Power

The branch certainly saw some interesting motive power over the years. At the turn of the last century five members of the Queen Class 2-2-2s, Nos. 1125/28/29/30/and 1132, which were built in 1875, were used at various times on the branch. Of these No. 1128 was allocated to Oxford from 1903 until its withdrawal in April 1914, and was the last surviving member of the class. Great Western 157 Class 2-2-2 No. 165 built in 1879 was also a regular performer on the branch until its withdrawal in December 1914. In 1906 both 165 and 1128 were fitted with ATC apparatus at Swindon in connection with the experimental use of this system on the branch. For over 50 years examples of the 455 Class 2-4-0T Metro locomotives saw use on both passenger and goods services. Their association with the branch ended when the last working Metro tank No. 3588 was withdrawn from Oxford in December 1949. However, by this date, the services were generally in the hands of ex-Great Western 5700 and 7400 Class 0-6-0PTs. The last passenger services were hauled on 16 June 1962 by ex-Great Western 5700 Class 0-6-0PT No. 3653 and ex-Great Western 2251 Class 0-6-0 No. 2221.

Yarnton was the junction station for the branch to Witney and Fairford. On 19 May 1962 Castle Class 4-6-0 No. 7006 *Lydford Castle* speeds through with a service from Paddington to Worcester and Hereford. The high level signal box which contained a 51 lever frame was opened on 13 June 1909. It was closed on 28 March 1971. (C. G. Stuart)

Oxford allocated 7400 class 0-6-0PT No. 7404 arrives at Witney on 19 May 1962 with the 08.23am service from Carterton to Oxford. (Michael Hale)

Another shot of No. 7404 as it stands at Lechlade on 14 May 1962 with the 12.44pm service from Oxford to Fairford. (C. G. Stuart)

Looking down from the road bridge at Lechlade on 11 June 1962 with on this occasion a 5700 class 0-6-0PT No. 3653 arriving on the 4.26pm service from Oxford. (A. E. Doyle)

Brize Norton and Bampton on 16 May 1959. The large airbase can be seen on the right. Standing in the down platform is Collett 2251 class 0-6-0 No. 2252 on a service to Fairford, in the up platform on a service to Oxford is 5700 class 0-6-0PT No. 9611. (C. G. Stuart)

Looking down from the road over- bridge at Fairford in 1959. 5700 class No. 9653 waits to depart with a three coach service to Oxford. (C. G. Stuart)

The small wooden engine shed at Fairford pictured here on 16 May 1959. On the left is Collett 2251 class 0-6-0 No. 2252 and alongside the water tower is 5700 class No. 0-6-0 No. 9653. Fairford was a sub shed of Oxford and closed in June 1962. The end of the branch is directly behind the shed. (C. G. Stuart)

Another 2251 class 0-6-0 No. 2221 stands at Witney during the last week of passenger services on the branch. The chalk inscription on the smoke box door reads 'The end is near travel before June 16th 1962'. Interestingly No. 2221 was allocated to Oxford for use on Witney branch services from January until July 1962. (C. G. Stuart)

A Swindon Cross Country class DMU comprising Nos W50679, W59271, W50727 stands at South Leigh station with the 'Isis' railtour on a snowy 14 February 1970. The LCGB tour started at Bristol and visited the Abingdon, Witney and Bicester branches amongst others. (C. G. Stuart)

This picture was taken on 11 November 1970 and shows the removal of the level crossing at Eynsham by the Oxfordshire Highways Department. (C. G. Stuart)

The Wycombe Railway

The Wycombe Railway Company was incorporated by an Act of Parliament on 27 July 1846 to construct a 9¾ mile single broad gauge line from the Great Western main line at Maidenhead to the Buckinghamshire town of High Wycombe. After a number of delays, mainly due to financing problems, the line opened for passenger traffic on 1 August 1854 and was worked from the start by the Great Western. The branch proved to be successful and on 28 June 1861 the Wycombe Railway Company obtained powers to extend the branch through to Aylesbury, and via a new junction station at Princes Risborough, to Oxford. The section between Wycombe and Thame was completed in July 1862, together with the intermediate station at Bledlow. After inspection the line opened for passenger traffic on 1 August 1862. The inaugural service, comprising three coaches, was hauled by the Gooch Sun Class 2-2-2 *Sunbeam* carrying Directors and shareholders. It arrived at Thame at 3pm 'to the great delight of the locals', who cheered its arrival. Regular passenger services comprising four a day in each direction were introduced between Thame and Paddington on Monday 4 August 1862. The short branch between Princes Risborough and Aylesbury was opened on 1 October 1863.

The branch left the Oxford to Didcot line at Kennington Junction. In 1958 Castle Class 4-6-0 No. 7007 *Great Western* passes Kennington Junction Signal Box with an up Worcester service. The 43 lever box opened in 1901 and unusually faced the branch. It was closed on 15 December 1973. (J. D. Edwards)

AEC diesel railcar No. 10 leaves the Thame branch at Kennington Junction with the 11.22am service from Princes Risborough to Oxford in January 1947. Notice the guard holding the single line totem. (Author's Collection)

Once Thame had been reached, thoughts turned to the remaining section between Thame and Kennington, where it would connect to the Didcot to Oxford main line via a new junction. Work started in December 1862; this section of the branch included two major engineering works, a 1,584ft tunnel between Wheatley and Horsepath (original spelling), and a 270ft bridge over the Thames just prior to the junction with the Great Western main line at Kennington. Work progressed well and both structures were completed during 1863. The new section was opened on 24 October 1864 and offered a second broad gauge route between Oxford and London. However, the broad gauge did not survive for long and on Tuesday 24 August 1870 the whole of the branch between Wycombe and Kennington Junction was closed for the conversion to narrow (standard) gauge. The whole exercise was completed in just eight days

with the line re opening for passenger traffic on Thursday 1 September 1870.

Initially stations were provided at Littlemore, Wheatley, Tiddington, Thame and Bledlow, with passing points together with up and down platforms at Thame and Wheatley. The station at Littlemore was situated on the down side; it had a single platform, with a brick built station building containing a ticket office and waiting room. There was a small yard and a coal siding that served the adjacent County Lunatic Asylum. At Wheatley the small station entrance building was also constructed in brick and stood on the up (Village) side of the line, access to the down platform being via the adjacent road bridge. The station at Tiddington stood on the down side and comprised a single platform and a wooden station building similar in style to Littlemore.

The station at Thame was a grander affair with a superb train shed designed by Pauling. This timber structure measured

A view of the single platform station at Littlemore taken around the turn of the last century. The signal box on the left was opened in 1892 and closed on 19 March 1951. The sidings here were used to supply coal to the County Lunatic Asylum, later Littlemore Psychiatric Hospital. (Author's Collection)

Morris Cowley station in the 1950s. The station was opened on 24 September 1928 and stood on the site of the Garsington Bridge Railmotor halt that was closed on 22 March 1915. (Author's Collection)

approximately 46ft wide by 90ft long and survived intact right up until the line was closed to passengers in 1963. As at Wheatley, the station entrance building was constructed of brick and was of a similar design. It also stood on the up (town) side; the up and down platforms being connected via a footbridge. As already mentioned the single platform station at Bledlow opened on 1 August 1862 and stood on the down side of the branch. The station building was constructed of brick and also incorporated the Stationmaster's house.

Signal boxes were situated on the branch at Littlemore. This box opened in 1891 and contained a 15 lever frame; it was closed on 19 February 1951. Morris Cowley was opened much later on 24 October 1928; it contained a 43 lever frame and was closed on 28 January 1982. The next box on the line was at Wheatley. This was another early box that contained 25 levers and was opened in March 1891; it was closed 12 July 1964. The small signal

box at Tiddington was also probably opened in March 1891. It contained a 15 lever frame and was reduced to a ground frame in around 1927. The box at Thame also dates from around 1891; it contained a 29 lever frame and was closed on 17 November 1968. The 16 frame box at Bledlow stood on the station platform; it was opened in November 1891 and closed on 15 September 1965.

The next stage in the development of services over the branch came with the opening of the Great Western and Great Central Joint line from Wycombe to Paddington on 2 April 1906. This now allowed passenger services to operate via Thame and Wycombe and then over the new more direct route to London rather than the old route via Bourne End and Maidenhead. The new route, at 56 miles, was actually 7½ miles shorter than the old route via Maidenhead. In 1897 the Great Western was looking to shorten the route between Paddington and Birmingham,

The sidings inside the Morris Motors (BMC) works at Cowley taken in 1962. The 0-4-0 Fowler Diesel Mechanical works shunter No. 4210101 can be seen on the right standing at the entrance to the large BMC parts building. (Laurence Johnston)

When the works diesel shunter was out of action the company would hire in a locomotive from Oxford (81F). On this occasion 4800 class 0-4-2T No. 1442 shunts a single wagon on the entrance siding. The works sidings were closed in 1976. (Laurence Johnston)

and one such proposal was to upgrade the Princes Risborough to Kennington Junction section of the old Wycombe Railway to form a new double-track main line. In anticipation of this in 1901 the Great Western replaced the 1874 built signal box at Kennington Junction by a new 43 lever box; the new box built facing the branch in anticipation of the branch upgrade. However, this proposal was abandoned in favour of the new cut-off route that was opened between Princes Risborough and Aynho Junction on 1 July 1910.

During this period, branch line passenger services were operated using Metro Class 2-4-0Ts and 517 Class 0-4-2Ts, with Armstrong Standard and Dean Goods Class 0-6-0s on many of the freight services. In February 1908 steam Railmotor services were introduced between Oxford and Thame. To accommodate the new services halts were opened at Hinksey

and Abingdon Road, and on the branch at Iffley, Garsington Road, and Horsepath. The services were very popular but were withdrawn on 22 March 1915 and were, surprisingly, not reinstated, with all of the halts being subsequently removed. In 1913 William Morris (Lord Nuffield) established his Morris Car factory at Cowley. From small beginnings the factory expanded over the ensuing years, and in 1927 the workforce at Cowley numbered 5,000. In 1914 a long siding was installed that connected the branch to the Morris works. It was used primarily for the conveyance of Mine Sinkers that were being produced in the original Cowley factory (formerly the Oxford Military College) as part of the war effort. Two extra sidings were also installed around the same time; these ran adjacent to the main line and served another part of the car factory that was being used for the production of munitions. With the rapid expansion of the Morris Motors and the adjacent Pressed Steel plant (which had opened its factory at Cowley in 1926) the Great Western opened a new station near the site of the old Garsington Bridge Halt on 24 September 1928, named somewhat appropriately Morris Cowley. Earlier in July 1928 a new larger goods yard was opened on the up side, together with additional sidings on the down side. By the early 1930s employment numbers at Cowley had risen to around 20,000. This workforce came from all parts of the county and beyond. In 1933 the Great Western introduced an early morning workman's train between Banbury and Morris Cowley: stopping at all stations *en route* it brought hundreds of workers each day to and from the Cowley factories.

During the winter months the Thames becomes a fast flowing river and at Kennington this resulted in subsidence of the railway bridge. This had been an ongoing problem for a number of years, and in 1922 and with heavier trains the Great Western decided to replace the original cast iron bridge with a completely new girder bridge. In order to keep the line open the new bridge was built alongside the original structure, with the whole exercise taking 15 months to complete due to the nature of the river at this point. The new bridge was opened for traffic on Sunday 29 July 1923. On completion the old bridge was removed but its brick abutments remain and can still be seen today.

To handle the goods traffic extensive sidings were built on both the up and down sides of the branch. Other sidings served the nearby Morris Car and Pressed Steel factories; these were all controlled by a new 31 lever frame 'Morris Cowley' signal box which was opened on

An unidentified Britannia Class 4-6-2 prepares to leave Morris Cowley yard in 1964 with the afternoon car service to Bathgate. On the left are the sidings to the Pressed Steel Plant and Nuffield Exports. (Author's Collection)

Horspath Halt was opened on 5 June 1933 and stood on the up side adjacent to the road bridge. A Railmotor halt was opened here on 1 January 1908, but closed 23 March 1915. The road bridge is still *in situ*, being saved from demolition by the local residents. (Author's Collection)

24 October 1928. The two factories had extensive sidings that ran from the branch; at Morris Cowley there were five sidings and a small locomotive shed for the two works locomotives. The Pressed Steel plant also had five sidings and a small shed for the two works shunters.

Two new halts were opened on the branch on 5 June 1933, at Horspath (later spelling) near the site of the 1905 Railmotor halt and at Towersey, east of Thame. During the 1920s many of the passenger services were being operated using Bulldog and County Class 4-4-0s; however, by the mid 1930s these had been replaced by 6100 Class 2-6-2Ts which were used on the branch right up until closure. AEC diesel railcars were first introduced on services over the branch in January 1935 and continued to be a regular feature until the railcar service was withdrawn in October 1957. The branch was classified as a 'Red' route by the Great Western, which restricted members of the King and 4700 Class locomotives from working on services between Princes Risborough and Oxford.

During the Second World War the branch gained extra importance when a military hospital was built at Holton Park near Wheatley. Regular hospital trains ran, usually from the Oxford direction, to Wheatley station, from where the injured were transferred in convoys of ambulances for the short trip up the hill to the hospital at Holton.

As with many other branch lines in the area, the use of the car resulted in a decline in passenger numbers, the Thame branch being no exception. From 6 January 1963 passenger services were withdrawn between Oxford and Princes Risborough, the last services being hauled by long serving Oxford 6100 Class 2-6-2Ts Nos. 6106 and 6111. The line remained open for freight and parcels traffic, and on 1 October 1963 a new car train was introduced between Morris Cowley and a new distribution centre at Bathgate in Scotland. The service was usually hauled by an Oxford based BR 9F 2-10-0, but on many occasions a Scottish based BR Britannia Class 4-6-2 was used.

For many years the branch had been used as a diversionary route for both passenger and freight services when the main line between Princes Risborough

BRITISH RAILWAYS

MORRIS MOTORS ATHLETIC & SOCIAL CLUB
MUSICAL FESTIVAL
AT
OXFORD

SATURDAY, SEPTEMBER 26th

FIRST AND SECOND CLASS
CHEAP DAY RETURN TICKETS

WILL BE ISSUED

TO

OXFORD

FROM ALL STATIONS AND HALTS WITHIN A RAIL DISTANCE OF

80 MILES

**TICKETS WILL BE AVAILABLE FORWARD AND
RETURN BY ANY TRAIN ON DAY OF ISSUE**

As certain trains are Second Class only, First Class passengers should, before booking, ascertain which trains are provided with First Class accommodation.

Notice as to Conditions.—These tickets are issued subject to the British Transport Commission's published Regulations and Conditions applicable to British Railways exhibited at their stations or obtainable free of charge at station booking offices. Luggage allowances are as set out in these general notices.

Tickets can be obtained in advance at Stations and Agencies

Further information will be supplied on application to Stations, Agencies, or to Mr. E. FLAXMAN, Commercial Officer, Paddington Station, W.2 (Telephone: Paddington 7000, Extension "Enquiries"; 8.0 a.m. to 10.0 p.m.), or to the Commercial Officer, Euston Station, N.W.1.

**Paddington and Euston Stations,
August 1959**

L.D. 528 D.   Printed by W. A. SMITH (Leeds) LTD., Carlton Printeries, Leeds.

A flyer advertising the famous Morris Motors music festival, held for many years at the Works Social club at Cowley. The Festival featured brass bands and choirs from around the country. The Morris Motors band was formed in 1924 and under the direction of Harry Mortimer it became one of the top brass bands in the country, winning many prizes. (Author's Collection)

Wheatley was one of the main passing points on the branch with both up and down platforms. The main station building is seen here in the 1920s. In the foreground is part of Avery's woodyard that operated at Wheatley from around 1880 right up until the line's closure. The whole site is now covered by a housing estate. (Author's Collection)

A service from Oxford arrives at Tiddington in July 1959, unusually hauled by 5600 class 0-6-2T No. 6664. On the left is the station signal box. Opened in 1907 with 15 levers, it was reduced to a ground frame in 1927. (Author's Collection)

and Aynho Junction was closed for engineering work. However the poor state of Horspath Tunnel and the high cost of repair (estimated at £60,000) ensured the closure of the line as a through route, with the centre section between Morris Cowley and Thame closing to all traffic on 1 May 1967. The line now became effectively two separate branches, Kennington Junction to Cowley, and Thame to Princes Risborough. The Thame section remained open to serve a BP oil terminal but when that closed in 1991, this section of the branch was closed and the track lifted. The branch to Cowley remained open to serve another BP Oil Terminal at Littlemore (closed in 1995) and the Morris and Pressed Steel plants. At Cowley a new road–rail freight terminal operated by F. C. Bennett was opened on 9 May 1984 on the site of the old down side goods shed. The old Morris Motors site was sold in 1992 and the factory and sidings were removed, being replaced by the Oxford Business Park. The Pressed Steel factory was, however, retained by BMW, being renamed 'Plant Oxford'. It is now the home of the Mini and at the time of writing the plant is producing around 1,000 cars

every 24 hours, of which 80 per cent are exported. The F. C. Bennett freight terminal was closed in 1997, together with the adjacent car loading sidings, and since then the whole area has been acquired by BMW for factory expansion.

The remains of the branch line from Kennington Junction currently serves a car loading terminal at the BMW Mini Plant. At the time of writing there are two services each day, operated by DB Schenker using WIA wagons. One service operates to Purfleet in Essex and another to Southampton Eastern docks; each train carries up to 280 cars in 50 double deck WIA wagons. At 660 metres in length these services are some of the longest in the country.

In recent years the local council, together with Chiltern Railways, have explored the re-opening of the Kennington Junction to Cowley section to passenger traffic. In 2016 Chiltern Railways operated a test train carrying local dignitaries from Oxford to Cowley, and if all goes to plan passenger trains should be running to Cowley, hopefully, within the next few years.

An early postcard view of Thame, showing the goods shed and sidings. (Author's Collection)

An auto service to Princes Risborough, hauled by 4800 class 0-4-2T No. 1437, auto coach W87 and with a four-wheeled parcels wagon, departs from Thame in the early 1950s. (Author's Collection)

Oxford allocated 6100 class 2-6-2T No. 6129 prepares to depart from Oxford on 6 May 1962 with the 4.45pm service to Princes Risborough. Oxford allocated 6100 class 2-6-2Ts worked services over the branch from the early 1930s right up until its closure in January 1963. (A. E. Doyle)

The 12.52 service from Oxford to Princes Risborough hauled by 6100 class 2-6-2T No. 6111 waits at a snowy Morris Cowley on 5 January 1963, this was the last weekend of passenger services over the branch. (C. G. Stuart)

The interior of the train shed at Thame taken on 28 March 1963 and just two months after the withdrawal of passenger services. Thame Station was designed by Pauling and opened with the first section of the branch between High Wycombe and Thame on 1 August 1862. In the background is the goods shed and on the right Thame signal box. (C. G. Stuart)

The signal box at Morris Cowley 'seen here in June 1980' was opened on 24 October 1928 and contained a 43 lever frame. It was closed on 28 January 1982. (Author)

6100 class 2-6-2T No. 6124 waits to depart from Bledlow with the 7.50am service from Oxford on 25 August 1962. The 16 lever frame signal box was opened in November 1891, and closed on15 September 1965.

An unidentified Western Class 52 diesel hydraulic passes the Blackbird Leys estate as it departs from Cowley with the afternoon 'cars' service to Bathgate. In the background is the Morris Motors car factory (at this time part of the British Motor Corporation). (Laurence Johnston)

The Oxford University Railway Society branch line railtour crosses the Thames bridge at Kennington on Sunday 18 May 1975. It is proposed to re-introduce a passenger service, possibly operated by Chiltern Railways, over the branch as far as the railhead at Cowley. (Peter Heath)

The remains of the old Thame branch now terminates at the Mini Plant at Cowley. The loading sidings are seen here on 21 July 2018 with a new Mini Cooper S being loaded onto the Morris Cowley to Southampton Eastern Docks service comprising 50 WIA double deck wagons. (Author)

This second shot shows another new Mini for export being loaded at what will be the front of the train. The 'Minis" as it is known locally runs down the branch to Hinksey yard, here the locomotive will run round the train in preparation for its journey to Southampton. A second 'Mini'service also operates on weekdays from Cowley to Purfleet. (Author)

The Blenheim and Woodstock Railway

Unlike the three other local branch lines, the Woodstock Railway was late on the scene, not opening until 19 May 1890. The Woodstock Railway was promoted by the 8th Duke of Marlborough, who put up most of the finance for the construction of the railway, and on its completion and until his death in 1892 was the Chairman of the Company. An interesting feature of the station at Woodstock was that for the whole of its working life it was named Blenheim for Woodstock, due of course to the input of money by the 8th Duke. The Act for the Woodstock Railway, for a 2½ mile branch that would connect with

the Oxford to Birmingham main line near Shipton-on-Cherwell, was passed on 25 September 1886. Construction of the branch started in 1888 but in March 1889 work stalled due to an issue regarding the junction with the Great Western main line at Shipton-on-Cherwell. It seems that the Great Western did not want Woodstock Railway services to operate over its main line to Woodstock Road (Woodstock Road was renamed Kidlington on the opening of the branch in May 1890). The problem was eventually resolved with the GWR insisting that the Woodstock Company build an extension to its branch to run alongside the main line and into a new bay platform at Woodstock Road station. The station at Woodstock Road had been officially opened by the Great Western on Friday 1 June 1855. Clinker's register of stations suggests it was opened as Langford Lane for a short period in 1855 but I can find no proof of this locally. To accommodate the branch services the down platform was extended by some 300ft in order to form a new bay. Unfortunately the Woodstock Company had not budgeted for the extra work and in order to get the branch finished the GWR financed the extension of the branch to Woodstock Road. Once completed, the branch was surveyed by Colonel F. H. Rich on 14 May 1890, and with 'all things being satisfactory' the Woodstock Railway was opened for business on Monday 19 May 1890. Initially there were five passenger trains each way on weekdays; there was no Sunday service. The branch was worked from the start by the Great Western, who supplied both locomotives and coaching stock. Even the first Stationmaster at

Woodstock, Albert Lofting, was a Great Western man who had previously been the Stationmaster at Woodstock Road.

In 1897 under the terms of the GWR Additional Powers Act the Woodstock Railway Company was purchased outright by the Great Western at a cost of £15,000. The 3¾ mile branch left the Great Western Oxford to Birmingham line at Kidlington, then ran adjacent to the main line for approximately 1 mile before branching away to cross both the Oxford Canal and the River Cherwell in quick succession before crossing the main road to Banbury (now the A4260). It then ran through a cutting and over open fields to the small town of Woodstock, where it terminated alongside the main Oxford to Chipping Norton Road (now the A44) almost opposite the main entrance of Blenheim Palace. The single platform terminus building at Woodstock was constructed of Cotswold stone with a slate roof in keeping with the rest of the

The beautifully kept station at Blenheim and Woodstock in the 1920s with the branch auto coach waiting in the platform. On the right is part of the station goods yard. (Author's Collection)

The 517 class 0-4-2T No. 1473 *Fair Rosamund* had a long association with the branch. It is pictured here in the bay at Kidlington with a service to Blenheim in 1932. It was built in May 1883 and allocated to Oxford. In 1896 it was named *Fair Rosamund*, and withdrawn in August 1935. (Author's Collection)

The auto-train service from Kidlington arriving at Blenheim for Woodstock hauled by 517 class 0-4-2T No. 830 on 13 June 1931. No. 830 was allocated to Banbury at this time and was probably on loan to Oxford as the regular branch locomotive No. 1473 was under repair. (Author's Collection)

The only intermediate station on the branch was Shipton-on-Cherwell Halt, which was opened on 1 April 1929, primarily to service the nearby cement works. The halt was situated adjacent to the roadbridge over the main road to Banbury (now the A4260); the entrance is seen here on the right. (Author's Collection)

town buildings. A small goods yard was provided together with a single-road engine shed. The whole terminus complex was controlled by a small signal box that stood adjacent to the engine shed.

Services to and from Kidlington comprised nine each way each weekday but by 1949 had reduced to eight each way, with the first service also running through from Oxford. The timetable also shows a mid-day service again running to and from Oxford; there was no Sunday service. However, often on Sundays excursions would operate to coincide with special events at the nearby Blenheim Palace. I can remember travelling with

my parents to a horse show at Blenheim Palace on a special Sunday service from Oxford in June 1953; the three coach train was hauled by 5400 Class 0-6-0PT No. 5413, and as I seem to recall, was quite full.

A certain amount of rationalisation took place at Woodstock with the closure of the signal box in 1926, being replaced by east and west ground frames. The engine shed was closed a year later on 17 June 1927 which resulted in the branch locomotive being serviced at Oxford, travelling each day on the first service which ran through from Oxford. On 1 April 1929 the Great Western

During 1935 the 517 class 0-4-2Ts were replaced on branch services by the new 4800 class 0-4-2Ts. Pictured here is No. 1442 on the branch auto-service at Shipton-on-Cherwell Halt in around 1952. (Author's Collection)

From early 1940 the services were also operated using the auto fitted 5400 Class 0-6-0PTs. No. 5413 with auto trailer No. 110 are pictured here on the early morning through service from Oxford to Blenheim for Woodstock, on 25 September 1948. This service delivered the daily fresh water supply to Wolvercot Junction Signal box. Here the signalman is collecting the water from the guard. (Mark Yarwood)

opened a halt adjacent to the Banbury Road bridge at Shipton-on-Cherwell. The halt served the nearby village and also the cement works at Bunkers Hill which had opened in June 1928. The line continued to operate with little change, but being in such close proximity to Oxford, and with both bus and car use increasing, passenger numbers declined and the branch was officially closed on Monday 1 March 1954, the last passenger service being the 6.48pm to Oxford on Saturday 27 February, hauled by 4800 Class 0-4-2T No. 1420. It was the last local branch line to open and the first to close. The branch may have gained more passengers and survived for a few years longer had the Western Region operated the Woodstock services to

and from Oxford, or even increased the connections at Kidlington.

In the years after closure approximately ½ mile of the branch from Kidlington northwards was used as a goods loop. The remains of the branch were lifted during March 1959. At Woodstock the old station and goods yard were purchased in 1960 by Messrs Youngs, who moved their garage and service station business from across the road to their new site. In 1965, part of the goods yard and adjacent track bed were sold to Blakes of Didcot for housing. I purchased my first house here in 1966. Youngs have now relinquished the site, but the original station building remains and is now in office use as part of a residential development that was constructed over the station site in 2013.

The last passenger service to Woodstock ran on Saturday 27 February 1954, the branch being closed from Monday 1 March. Seen here arriving at Shipton-on-Cherwell Halt is the last passenger service, hauled by 4800 class 0-4-2T No. 1420. (G. Hine)

The Woodstock station building after closure and before conversion to Young's garage and filling station, circa 1958. (Michael Hale)

Motive Power

The branch was always worked by small tank engines using the auto-train system, usually 517 Class 0-4-2Ts, and in later years auto-fitted 5400 Class 0-6-0s and 4800 Class 0-4-2Ts. For a short time in the period before the First World War the Great Western also operated a steam Railmotor service between Oxford and Woodstock. One member of the 517 Class had a long association with the Woodstock branch. No. 1473 was built at Wolverhampton in May 1883 and by 1892 it was working from Oxford,

soon becoming the regular locomotive on the Woodstock branch. In February 1896 it was named *Fair Rosamund* after Rosamund Clifford, an interesting choice for a name as Rosamund, who apparently lived in a 'bower' near Woodstock, was the mistress of King Henry II. On 31 March 1896 the 9th Duke returned to Blenheim after marrying Consuelo Vanderbilt in New York, and No. 1473, newly named, was used to haul the branch service. No. 1473 continued to work regularly on the branch for the next 39 years until its withdrawal in August 1935.

In this second picture the platform contains a variety of vehicles stored under the canopy. (Michael Hale)

This view shows the old station being converted into Young's garage and filling station. The garage was originally situated on the opposite side of the road but moved to this new and larger site during 1960. (C. G. Stuart)

Chapter 5

THE GREAT WESTERN ENGINE SHEDS

When the railway arrived at Oxford in June 1844, locomotives used on the branch were serviced at Didcot, where a single-road brick built shed and turntable were provided. At the Oxford terminus basic coal and watering facilities were certainly provided and probably a locomotive turntable. Unfortunately the lack of detailed track diagrams makes it difficult to know the exact layout of the yard.

In October 1850 the line was extended north to Banbury via Millstream Junction and, as at Oxford, it is probable that only basic servicing facilities were provided at Banbury. The main change came on 1 October 1852 when the line was opened through to Birmingham. It was around this time that a new broad gauge shed was opened at Oxford. This two-road shed stood at the north end of the up platform. It was constructed of wood and measured approximately 200ft in length; the loco yard contained a 25ft turntable together with rudimentary coaling and watering facilities. Water was obtained from a well that was, and still is, situated at the south end of the up platform, water being stored in a large tank that was situated above the steam pump house. The Gooch engine record sheets indicate that on 18 February 1854 eight locomotives were working from

Oxford. The highest number recorded was in March 1861, when the records show that 16 locomotives were at Oxford, plus two at Abingdon.

However, the increasing number of standard gauge services operating in the area saw the broad gauge allocation plummet, and by 1863 the number of locomotives shown as working at Oxford was down to just seven. This number remained pretty much static until the broad gauge was removed north of Oxford on 1 April 1869, after which date only three broad gauge locomotives are shown at Oxford, with another at Abingdon. Those at Oxford were probably used on freight traffic and to shunt the goods yard at the old Grandpont station. On 25 November 1872 broad gauge working was removed south of Oxford, resulting in the closure of the broad gauge shed, together with the yard at Grandpont. The building remained in use as a standard gauge carriage shed, probably until 1879 when it was demolished to allow for alterations and improvements to the sidings.

The second engine shed at Oxford was constructed on land to the north of the new station and adjacent to the down main line at Cripley Meadow. The first shed on this site was built by the Oxford, Worcester & Wolverhampton Railway Company, who had started to

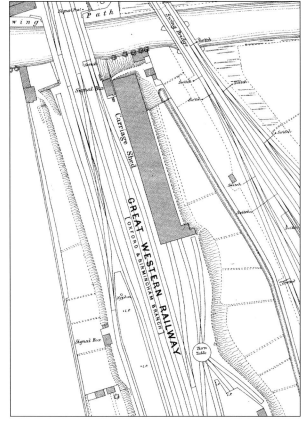

Gooch 'Iron Duke' Class 4-2-2 Hirondelle is pictured here at Oxford in around 1862. In the background is the Broad Gauge engine shed. It was probably closed after the removal of of broad gauge north of Oxford in 1869. Hirondelle was built at Swindon in Decenber 1848 and withdrawn in May 1873. (Author's Collection)

Map of the site of the broad gauge locomotive shed and sidings, seen here in 1876 when in use as a carriage shed. Also shown is the position of the original Oxford 'B' signal box. (Ordnance Survey)

The wooden engine shed at Oxford pictured here in 1921. The three-road shed dates from around 1862, and the single-road extension which became No. 4 road was added in 1866. (Author's Collection)

Metro 2-4-0T No. 1461 stands alongside the coaling stage at Oxford on 13 March 1926. Oxford had an allocation of Metros for many years. They were used on services to Fairford and also to Princes Risborough. No. 1461 was built in April 1882 and was allocated to Oxford from March 1921 until its withdrawal in August 1930. (Author's Collection)

run standard gauge services into Oxford in June 1853. This was a single-road standard gauge shed and is described as being constructed of wood with a slated gable style roof; it stood just to the north of the Sheepwash Channel. It was opened for use on 1 April 1854, together with an engine turntable and coal and water facilities. Although not highly detailed, the 1854 Cholera map of Oxford shows a small shed on this site. In October 1861 the Great Western introduced standard gauge services between Paddington and Birmingham via Banbury, and to Worcester and Wolverhampton via the West Midland lines. At this time the only standard gauge locomotive facilities at Oxford were provided at what was now the West Midland Railway shed. On 1 July 1861, under a lease agreement, the Great Western took over the working of West

Midland services, and some two years later the Great Western Railway (by the West Midland Railway Act of 13 July 1863) purchased the West Midland Company. The initial working arrangement now gave the Great Western control of the West Midland facilities at Oxford, and with the increase in Great Western standard gauge passenger and freight services it soon became evident that the ex-OW&WR shed and servicing facilities were inadequate. This resulted in the old single-road shed being demolished and replaced by a larger three-road shed on the same site. It was previously assumed that it was the ex-OW&WR single road shed that stood alongside the newer three-road Great Western shed. That is clearly not the case as evidence of a new single-road extension to the existing shed is provided in a report by William Armstrong on 2 May 1866 to

Regular Woodstock branch locomotive 517 Class 0-4-2T No. 1473 *Fair Rosamund* stands in the shed yard at Oxford in 1930. The shed foreman's office can be seen on the right. (P. J. Reed/GWT)

the Locomotive Carriage and Permanent Way Committee, regarding the provision of 'additional shed accommodation at various locations on the system'. Within this report is the recommendation that 'accommodation for eight additional engines was required at Oxford', with the estimated cost put at £1,800. Accordingly the 'extension to the engine shed at Oxford' was approved on 18 April 1866 at a cost of £1,820. The new single-road extension was constructed during August 1866 and was situated alongside the three-road shed and adjacent to the down main line. Looking at the topography of the area it would have been impossible to construct the extension on the other side of the existing three-road building due to the closeness of the nearby Fiddlers Island stream. The 1878 OS map shows that the two buildings were exactly the same

length, 240ft, and with the provision of an extra road the whole structure was around 75ft wide. Contemporary photographs clearly show that both buildings were almost identical in design, constructed of wood with slated gable style roofs. The opening side windows were exactly the same on both buildings, and interestingly, for the whole of its working life the single-road extension was known as No. 4 road.

The main shed building included a store room and foreman's office, and to the north of the building stood a pump house, a carpenters' shop, a fitters' shop, a blacksmiths' shop and what is described as a repairing shed. This latter building contained a lifting crane and was entered via a 45ft turntable. The yard also contained a water tank and a separate coaling shed, while a small

Some of the shed staff pose for the camera on Southern King Arthur Class 4-6-0 No. 765 *Sir Gareth* in 1937. From L to R back row: R. Betts, C. Parsons. Middle row: C. Turner, R. Field, K. Hale, L. Jackson, F. Freestone, W. Ponsford, J. Sanwell. W. Boodell, C. Woodley. The Southern driver is unknown. (Author's Collection)

coaling platform containing two cranes stood between the two. In 1895 the old repair shop was rebuilt into a single-road building with a new 24,000 gallon water tank constructed above the entrance. The new tank was still fed from the nearby Thames via the pump house, but in later years from the mains. On 21 May 1931 approval was given for extending the lifting shop at a cost of £1,400 and for the provision of a new 50 ton chain hoist supplied by Royce Ltd at a cost of £496. At the same time the siding serving the lifting shop was altered. Some years earlier the old turntable had been removed and relocated adjacent to the Thames in an area known locally as 'the field'. Initially a 55ft turntable was provided, but with locomotives becoming larger and longer, it was replaced in 1906 by a new 65ft Ransomes Rapier turntable that served the shed for the next 60 years.

In 1884 a new coaling stage, served by a ramp, was constructed on the site of the old coaling shed. The new stage was constructed of wood and provided a greatly improved coaling capacity. An unfortunate feature of the coaling plant was its low coaling height, ideal for a 3,000 or 3,500 gallon tender but quite useless for the taller 4,000 gallon tenders that were progressively being fitted to many of the new 4-6-0s. Locos fitted with these larger tenders were coaled at Oxford using a separate coaling crane, not an ideal solution for a busy shed. The coaling plant suffered much wear and tear over the years, and photographs show that it had been extensively patched up using corrugated iron sheets. In 1906 the Great Western was considering a scheme to upgrade the facilities at Oxford with the provision of a roundhouse and new coaling plant, but for whatever reason this never happened; two other similar proposals in the 1920s and '30s were also dropped.

In 1908/9 the down platform at Oxford was extended northwards; this required alterations to the trackwork and the provision of a new span over the Sheepwash Channel bridge. In order to provide the new connection, the south end of No. 4 road at the shed was shortened by around 80ft.

The Second World War saw major alterations to the shed yard. Under the wartime Transport Finance Plan the old coaling plant was replaced by a new and much larger double-sided coaling plant; constructed of concrete it was now capable of dealing with the largest of locomotives. To achieve this the old North goods yard adjacent to the Cripley Meadow allotments was removed. The whole site was remodelled to provide much better access to the shed and the new coaling plant. The 65ft turntable that had been installed in 1906 was retained and new connecting sidings were installed. The subsequent removal of the old coaling plant also allowed the locomotive sidings to be extended. The new layout now allowed locomotives to enter the shed yard via a new north entrance at Walton Well, while also at the north end new sidings were provided for the shed's emergency coal supply. The total cost of the remodelling work was put at £48,735. The loss of the old goods yard was easily absorbed with the construction during 1942 of a new and much larger yard south of Oxford at Hinksey. The closure of the ex-LNWR shed at Rewley Road in December 1950 saw ex-LMS and LNER locomotives arriving from the Bletchley branch use the facilities at the ex-Great Western shed. A long siding known locally as Attwood's siding that ran alongside the adjacent allotments was used for many years to stable locomotives that had worked in from Bletchley. The siding was named after one Tommy Attwood who was a popular member of the shed staff. Over the years the old wooden

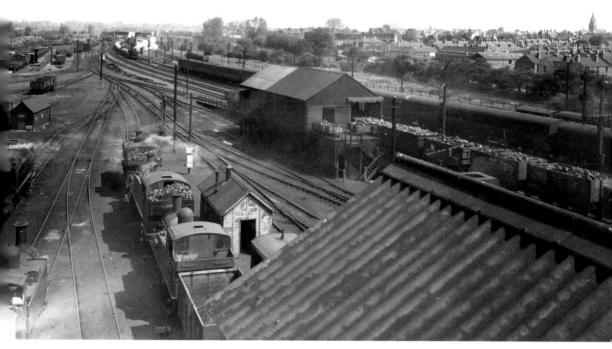

A view of the yard from the top of the lifting shop in 1941 shows to good effect the old coaling plant that was removed during the remodelling work in November 1944. (Author's Collection)

AEC diesel railcar No. W3W stands outside the works at Oxford in 1954. Railcars were allocated to Oxford from 1935 until 1957 mainly for Thame branch services. For many years a mechanical fitter was stationed at Oxford for Railcar repairs. No. W3W was built in July 1934; it was allocated to Oxford in November 1953 until its withdrawal in March 1955. (Author's Collection)

shed building had remained basically intact, but in 1960 the roof was replaced, and in 1963 major alterations took place when new offices were constructed at the back end of the shed building. This required the removal of the south end of the shed, which resulted in the shed facilities being somewhat reduced. In this guise the building and yard continued to be used by both steam and diesel locomotives, until officially closed to steam on 31 December 1966. The building saw use for a few days longer as more and more withdrawn locomotives arrived for storage, and on 3 January 1966 Modified Hall Class 4-6-0 No. 6998 *Burton Agnes Hall* was steamed up and used to haul the last official steam-hauled train from Oxford to Banbury. After closure, two 5700 Class 0-6-0PTs, Nos. 9773 and 9789, were used to move some of the large number of redundant locomotives around the yard. I have been reliably informed by an ex-Oxford driver that No. 9789 was actually the last ex-Great Western locomotive to be used. In the early months

On the morning of 5 September 1957 ex-LMS 8F 2-8-0 No. 48417 fell into the turntable pit at Oxford. Subsequently the turntable was out of use until 11 October; many locomotives were turned at Yarnton or on the Yarnton loop. Pictured here in September 1957 being turned at Yarnton is Bulleid Pacific No. 34093 *Saunton*. (G. Coleman)

of 1966 No. 6998 was stored at Oxford after its purchase by the Great Western Society. On 2 April 1966 it was once again steamed up and left the shed for its new home at Totnes. It was fitting that the last steam working from the shed was a Hall. The class had a long association with Oxford, and between 1931 and 1965 some 91 different members of the class were allocated to the shed.

The last shed foreman was the late Joe Tretheway, a Cornishman who had started as a fireman at St Blazey shed in 1935. After moving around the system he became the foreman at Oxford in

1960, and when the shed closed he had the distinction of being the last ex-Great Western shed foreman at an ex-Great Western shed. The shed continued to be used by diesel locomotives until 1967 when the old wooden building, lifting shop and turntable were removed. In July 1968 many of the remaining sidings were removed and a small refuelling bay and stabling point for main line diesels was constructed on the site. Interestingly, the shed water tank that stood above the old lifting shop was retained. The new refuelling point continued in use until August 1984 after

A high level view of the shed yard taken from the coaling plant on 20 July 1963. (C. P. Walker)

On 3 January 1966 Modified Hall Class 4-6-0 No. 6998 *Burton Agnes Hall* worked the 2.20pm Bournemouth to Newcastle service as far as Banbury, after which it was sold to the Great Western Society. After some months in store at Oxford it departed under its own steam to Totnes Quay. It is pictured here on 2 April 1966 being prepared to depart for Totnes. (Author's Collection)

which date locomotive refuelling moved to Reading. The site was soon cleared, although the water tank remained *in situ* until it was removed in 1992. The 1963 office building survived for some years housing 'Turbo Ted's nursery'. In recent years the old building has been demolished and replaced by a much more modern structure currently operated by Co-operative Child Care as the 'Oxford Station Nursery'. The remains of the old shed yard now comprise a small engineers' yard and three stabling sidings, but much of the area is now covered by a large development of Oxford University

flats for postgraduate students. This whole area is now accessed via a new road that was built in 1970 on the site of the old Cripley Road carriage sidings. In 2001 it was named Roger Dudman Way, after a former Lord Mayor of Oxford. In 2018 the old carriage sidings on the up side, known locally as Jericho sidings and used for many years for stabling DMUs, have been completely relaid in preparation for the introduction of the new 769/9 units, and eventually, one hopes, electric units. To make the sidings more user friendly the five sidings have been fitted with ground level lighting and driver walkways.

Castle Class 4-6-0 No. 7029 *Clun Castle* from Old Oak Common stands in the yard at Oxford in August 1962. The Castle is now preserved in running order at Tyseley. (C. G. Stuart)

Southall based 9F 2-10-0 No. 92207 in the yard at Oxford, June 1963. On the right is 4800 Class 0-4-2T No. 1444. (C. G. Stuart)

Oxford always had a good allocation of Hall Class locomotives with up to 17 at any one time working from the depot. They were used on both passenger and freight services. Standing on No. 2 coaling plant in March 1962 is No. 4979 *Wootton Hall*. Also in the line awaiting coaling are a 2800 2-8-0, an ex-LMS 8F 2-8-0 and another Hall. (C. G. Stuart)

Southall-allocated 2800 Class No. 2841 stands in the yard at Oxford on 22 March 1962. (C. G. Stuart)

Ex-LMS locomotives were daily visitors. Here Class 5 No. 44981 takes water at Oxford MPD on 22 March 1962 after working in from the Bletchley line. (C. G. Stuart)

For many years Oxford had an allocation of up to three ex-Great Western 7200 Class 2-8-2Ts. Here No. 7209 stands in the yard at Oxford on 22 March 1962. (C. G. Stuart)

Ex-Southern Railway Battle of Britain Class 4-6-2 No. 34057 *Biggin Hill* stands in the shed yard at Oxford on 25 August 1965. (David Green)

No. 34104 *Bere Alston* moves onto the turntable at Oxford in preparation for its return journey to Bournemouth, 25 August 1965. (David Green)

The smoky interior of No. 4 road at the shed in April 1965. In view is Hymek No. D7062, an ex-LMS Ivatt 2-6-0 and a Hall Class 4-6-0. (Author)

A view of the yard full of withdrawn locomotives taken on 1 January 1966. An ex-LMS 8F No. 48287 is seen passing on the main line with an up Esso oil train. (A. E. Doyle)

Western Class Diesel Hydraulic No. D1020 *Western Hero* stands in the yard at Oxford in 1963. It had previously broken down and was waiting repair. (Author's Collection)

Warship Class Diesel Hydraulic No. D835 *Pegasus* is pictured here at Walton Well in the summer of 1969. On the cab step is carriage shunter George Dussold; the Old Oak Common driver is not identified. (A. E. Doyle)

After the steam depot was demolished a small refuelling and stabling point was constructed on the site. This remained in use until August 1984 when refuelling facilities were switched to Reading, after which the sidings became an occasional stabling point. The disused fuelling plant is seen here in February 1991, with two Class 47s and a Class 08. The water tank that stood above the old steam lifting shop was removed in 1992. (A. E. Doyle)

Still in Scot Rail livery but now operated by Network South East, Class 47 No. 47635 stands in the stabling sidings at Oxford on 19 September 1986. (David Benyon)

Chapter 6

SIGNALLING AT OXFORD

When the Oxford branch opened in June 1844 it would have been operated on the time interval system, with the various sidings and signals being operated by switchmen using hand operated points. Signals at this time were of the disc and crossbar type, but over the ensuing years these were gradually replaced by semaphore signals. During the 1870s the Great Western introduced signal boxes in the Oxford area with the result that many of the switchmen became signalmen.

Information on these early boxes is sparse; the 1878 Ordnance Survey map of the Oxford station area shows that it was controlled by four signal boxes, all of which would have been constructed of wood. The first of these was Oxford 'D', which stood approximately half a mile south of the station on the down side of the line and controlled access to the south end yard. It was replaced in 1894 by the 'Oxford South' box; this box which had a 25 lever frame was closed in March 1942 and replaced with a new 69 lever frame brick-built box at Hinksey North.

Oxford 'C' or Oxford Goods Shed was situated on the down side immediately south of the Botley Road Bridge and adjacent to the level crossing. It was replaced in January 1908 with a new larger box that contained a 47 lever frame.

In 1942 under wartime conditions the outside of the frame room was protected from potential bomb damage by a brick lining and probably at the same time it was renamed Oxford Station South.

Oxford 'B' was constructed in around 1874 and stood adjacent to the up sidings and south of the Sheepwash Channel bridge. It was closed in around 1900 and subsequently removed to allow for the extension of the up platform. It was replaced by a new box that was constructed on the north side of the Sheepwash Channel bridge; named Oxford Engine Shed it contained a 97 lever frame and was the largest signal box in the Oxford area. In 1942 it was renamed Oxford Station North and around the same time the frame room was also brick lined.

Oxford 'A' stood to the north of the station, just south of the Walton Well Road overbridge. This was another early wooden box; it was replaced in November 1894 by Oxford North, a new larger box containing a 34 lever frame. This box was closed in November 1940 and replaced by a new box at Oxford North Junction, constructed of brick and with an 88 lever frame. It controlled the newly opened North Junction that connected the LMSR Bletchley branch to the Great Western main line.

Apart from those mentioned above, signal boxes were also situated south of

Looking north in 1953. On the left the down signals control access to the loco yard, the loop and the down main. The others are the up main, platform 1 and bay backing signals. On the left is the loco shed and on the right Oxford Station North Box. The box was opened in September 1896 and contained a 100 lever frame. It was initially named Oxford Engine Shed but was renamed Station North in 1944. It was closed under the Oxford MAS scheme on 7 October 1973. Also on the right an up service waits to depart from the Jericho carriage sidings. (Author's Collection)

During1959 the individual signal posts were replaced by this large gantry that straddled the tracks. The gantry was a feature at Oxford until its removal in 1975 when it was replaced by MAS. (Author)

Castle Class 4-6-0 No. 5018 *St Mawes Castle* departs from Oxford with a semi-fast service to Paddington on 15 August 1959. On the left is Oxford Station South box, opened in May 1908 as Oxford Goods Shed, replacing an earlier box on the same site. It was re-named Station South in 1942. It was closed under the Oxford MAS scheme on 7 October 1973 but was used for a few years as a store prior to its demolition in 1979. (J. D. Edwards)

Wolvercot siding signal box; the box was opened in June 1900 and contained a 29 lever frame. It was closed on 7 November 1962. The level crossing gave entry to Port Meadow; a siding here contained a small goods platform that was used for many years for the delivery of paper and pulp to the nearby paper mill. (J. D. Edwards)

Oxford at: Appleford Crossing (22 levers); Culham (19 levers); Radley (43 levers); and at Kennington Junction (43 levers). North of Oxford there were boxes at: Wolvercot Siding (29 levers); Wolvercot Junction (35 levers); Kidlington (51 levers) and on the Worcester line at Yarnton Junction (51 levers). Notice that this time the Great Western boxes were known as Wolvercot, instead of the later Wolvercote.

During the Second World War new boxes were opened at: Sandford (34 levers) on 7 April 1940; at Nuneham (6 levers) on 15 December 1940; at Hinksey South (72 levers) on 29 March 1942 and at Hinksey North (58 levers) on 5 April 1942.

The 1960s saw the start of rationalisation in the Oxford area, with the closure of many of the wartime loops together with the local branch lines and sidings. This also resulted in the closure of a number of the ex-Great Western boxes. The first to close was Nuneham Box on 18 October 1953, then Culham on 12 January 1961, Sandford on 14 December 1964, followed by Radley on 23 May 1965, and Appleford Crossing which was closed and reduced to a ground frame on 17 May 1965. On the main line north of Oxford, Wolvercot Siding was closed on 7 November 1962, Kidlington on 16 September 1968, Yarnton Junction on 28 March 1971 and Wolvercot Junction on 14 October 1973.

Rationalisation also took place on the ex-LNWR line out of Oxford. The signal

The ex-LNWR signal box at Rewley Road was opened in 1883 and contained a 36 lever frame. It was closed on 31 July 1959, after which it was reduced to a ground frame. Also in view is the large Oxford Station North Box. (J. D. Edwards)

No book on Oxford would be complete without a picture of the unique Western Region up starter upper quadrant signal at Oxford North junction. Built at Caversham signal works it was installed by the Western Region in 1950 as an experiment, but remained in use until its removal in October 1973. It is now on display in the National Railway Museum York. (Author's Collection)

The LMS signal box at Oxford Port Meadow was opened on 29 March 1942; it contained a 30 lever frame and controlled the wartime goods loops. It was closed on 28 August 1960. (Author's Collection)

box at Rewley Road was closed on 31 July 1959. Port Meadow Signal Box, which had been opened on 14 December 1941, was closed on 28 August 1960, followed by the small box at Islip on 13 December 1962. Banbury Road Junction was closed on 14 October 1973 together with Bicester No. 2 box which had opened on 9 November 1941. Bicester No. 1 that controlled the nearby level crossing was closed on 9 June 1986.

The end of the remaining manually operated signal boxes in the Oxford area came during October 1973 when semaphore signalling was removed and replaced by Multiple Aspect Signalling (MAS), with the whole area being controlled by the Oxford Panel. This small power box was situated on the down platform and was brought into use on 7 October 1973.

In July 2018 the long running Oxford signalling project, under the direction of Network Rail, was completed. Amongst the work carried out was the removal of the old MAS signalling system and the erection of a number of signal gantries north and south of the station, together with the installation of bi-directional signalling between Appleford and Heyford using high visibility LED signals. The down goods loop which was opened in 1942 and removed in 1976 was reinstated and is designated 'The Down Oxford Relief Line'. This runs alongside Port Meadow between Oxford and Wolvercote

The interior of the Oxford power box taken on 11 June 2018. Opened on 7 October 1973, it was closed on 28 July 2018 when all signalling operations in the Oxford area were switched to the Thames Valley Signalling Centre at Didcot. (Author)

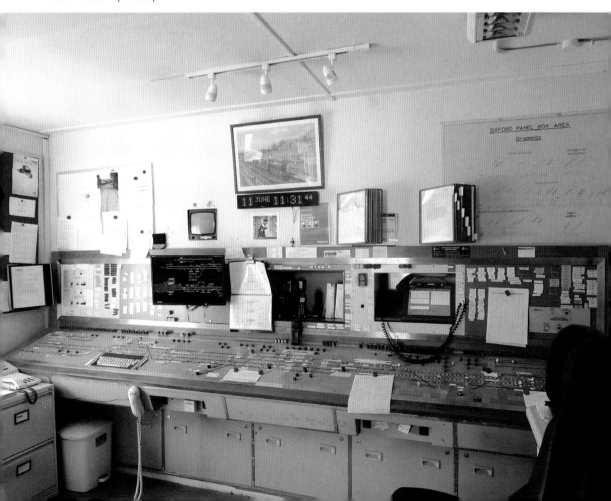

and has increased both passenger and freight capacity north of Oxford. The new signalling system has resulted in the closure of the 1973 MAS power box at Oxford, and from 23 July 2018 all signalling operations were switched to the new Thames Valley Signalling Centre at Didcot. The signalling centre, which was opened in 2010, has since June 2018 been using a new digital Traffic Management system and now controls the main line between Didcot and Heyford, together with the Cotswold line as far as Ascot-under-Wychwood. Much work was also carried out at Oxford North Junction to provide a double track between Oxford and Oxford Parkway, which together with bi-directional working will provide extra capacity, currently for Chiltern Trains but also in the future for East West rail services to Bletchley, Milton Keynes and beyond. The new signalling system and the new track layout has allowed a better regulation of passenger and freight trains passing through the Oxford area; which in turn has resulted in increased line speeds and better timekeeping for passengers and freight alike.

The large relay room was situated under the power box; it is pictured here on 11 June 2018. (Author)

Chapter 7

THE GOODS DEPARTMENT

Goods traffic has formed an important part of railway operations at Oxford right from the opening of the Oxford Railway in 1844. Its importance was such that the goods shed was actually the largest building at the Grandpont terminus. During these early years the Great Western's revenue from goods traffic was actually greater than that from passenger traffic. The first services to and from Oxford comprised mixed trains with large amounts of coal and livestock being moved. The expansion of the Oxford branch through to the industrial midlands in 1852 saw a considerable increase in the amount of goods being carried. It was also at this time that the old terminus at Grandpont was closed to passengers and effectively became Oxford South goods yard. The mixing of the gauge south of Oxford in 1856 allowed goods trains

The goods yard at Becket Street with a line of empty cattle wagons. The yard was established in around 1856, when livestock were unloaded here and moved on the hoof to the Cattle Market in Gloucester Green. This rather inconvenient manoeuvre ended when in 1932 the cattle market at Gloucester Green was moved to a new location at nearby Oxpens Road. The Oxpens cattle market was closed in 1979. (Minn collection Bodleian Library)

A view of the South Goods depot at Oxford in 1930 with both horse drawn and mechanical vehicles in view. The main building had three main loading bays, and on the right the depot weighbridge can be seen. In the years before closure the building was used as a parcels depot. The weighbridge and building remained in use until 1986. (Author's Collection)

to travel for long distances without the problem of gauge interchange, the 5.30pm service from Exeter to Birmingham and the 2.00pm Basingstoke to Manchester being two early examples. Another service inaugurated in 1856 ran between Basingstoke and Victoria Basin in Wolverhampton, and was still operating in the 1950s. The growth of goods services locally continued through the latter half of the nineteenth century. In 1858 there were 49 goods trains passing through Oxford daily and by the early 1900s this figure had increased to almost 100.

Much of this increase was due to the opening of the GW/GC connection at Banbury Junction. This resulted in a considerable increase in coal traffic, both passing through and using the small

yards at Oxford, which at this time were situated at Beckett Street and Oxford North. A small standard gauge goods yard comprising just five sidings and a cattle dock had been established at Becket Street probably soon after the introduction of the narrow gauge south of Oxford in 1856. The old south goods yard at Grandpont, which had never been converted to mixed gauge, was closed when the broad gauge was removed south of Oxford in 1872. With the gradual increase in goods traffic, facilities were extended with the construction of further sidings and a large goods shed south of the Osney Lane footbridge, to form Oxford South End yard. The yard here was gradually extended and by the 1930s comprised 15 sidings. The goods yard at Oxford North was first established

Oxford North goods yard seen here in 1942. The yard was removed during the Autumn of 1944 to allow for the expansion of the locomotive depot. On the left foreground is the depot reserve coal supply. In the background are the Cripley Meadow allotments, these date from around 1891 when the land was leased to the North Oxford and Jericho Allotments Association. The allotments are still in use today. (Authors Collection)

Ivatt Class 4 2-6-0 No. 43003 on a class F coal empties from Hinksey to Swanbourne yard crosses from the Western Region to the London Midland Region at Oxford North Junction on 26 May 1952. These inter-regional services were a feature of freight traffic through Oxford. (G.D. Parkes)

in the 1890s and initially contained nine sidings, and in 1932 it was enlarged with the addition of a further eight sidings. The Becket Street and South End yards were used mainly for general goods and parcels traffic, with much of the coal traffic being handled at Oxford North yard.

It is difficult today to comprehend the amount of coal traffic arriving in the City by rail. Coal was an important commodity and probably every household at this time burned coal. In 1911 there were 27 coal/coke dealers and agents, with a further 45 coal and coke merchants operating in the Oxford area. If you factor in the requirement for coal to supply the Great Western and to a lesser extent the LNWR locomotive depots then thousands of tons of coal were being delivered by rail to Oxford each week. I can well remember the smog that was a result of burning coal as a fuel. The Government's answer was the introduction of the 1956 Clean Air Act, which promoted the use of smokeless fuels, together with gas and electricity. This resulted in a sharp decline in the use of coal and by the early 1970s only seven coal merchants were operating locally. Today there are just two, both general dealers in all fuels. It is interesting to reflect that much of the younger population of this country have probably never encountered coal. Many of the schoolchildren who visit the railway centre at Didcot, when shown a piece of coal, have no idea what it is.

A considerable amount of coal arriving at Oxford also supplied the gas works at St Ebbes. The works had been opened by the Oxford Gas, Light, and Coke Company in 1818. Over the years and with the increasing use of gas in the City the works were expanded, eventually covering an area of 19 acres, and producing some 3 million cubic ft of gas per day. The works had its own

Ex-Great Western 4300 class 2-6-0 No. 6321 with an up class H mixed freight from the Banbury line at Wolvercot Junction, 25 September 1948. The tender is lettered 'British Railways'. (M. Harwood)

ROD Class 2-8-0 No. 3048 slowly makes its way through Oxford on 18 September 1949 with a class E freight service from the midlands to Hinksey Yard. (Author's Collection)

private sidings, with coal being delivered from the adjacent Great Western main line via an exchange siding. During the winter months the works received one coal train each day from either South Yorkshire or Derbyshire. For many years the extensive gasworks sidings were shunted using small Peckett and Bagnall 0-4-0STs. The works, which had been taken over by the Southern Gas Board in 1948, were closed in 1960 and finally demolished in 1968. Today natural gas is supplied via pipeline from Southampton feeding a large gas holder at Cowley.

The various goods yards at Oxford remained pretty much unchanged until the start of the Second World War, when extensive work was undertaken to upgrade the capacity of the railway locally. With Oxford being such an important railway hub the outbreak of war resulted in the provision of new junctions, sidings and yards. The first major change took place with the construction of Oxford North Junction; this was an important junction that connected the Great Western main line to

the ex-LNWR Bletchley branch. It opened, together with a new 'Oxford North Junction' signal box, on 3 November 1940, and around the same time a 40,000 gallon water tower was constructed just to the south of the new junction and adjacent to the up relief line. The new junction allowed freight and other traffic to travel from the south to the east, thus avoiding London altogether. Prior to its opening freight traffic was exchanged between Rewley Road and the Great Western line via a 22-wagon capacity exchange siding. To the north of Oxford at Yarnton additional exchange sidings together with a 65ft locomotive turntable were installed and brought into use on 20 August 1940. The opening of a new ordnance depot at Bicester during 1941/2 greatly increased the traffic on the ex-LNWR line. In order to handle the additional trains over this section a new signal box and two additional goods loops were opened at Port Meadow on 14 December 1941.

The dead end layout of the old yard at Oxford North precluded its use as an exchange yard for goods services.

The same applied to both of the south yards, so in order to increase capacity a new yard was opened about a mile south of Oxford at Hinksey during July and August 1942. Hinksey comprised up and down yards and had a capacity for around 1,000 wagons. It was controlled by two new signal boxes, Hinksey North which opened on 5 April 1942, and Hinksey South which opened slightly earlier on 29 March 1942. This new yard allowed a greater amount of goods traffic to be sorted locally and was soon being shunted 24 hours each day. In November 1944 improvements were made to the Great Western locomotive depot which entailed the removal of Oxford North goods yard. This allowed the construction of a new double-sided coaling plant, and the enlargement of the locomotive yard and servicing facilities.

During the early years of the war the lines in the area often reached saturation point, and to cope with the extra wartime traffic, during April 1942 the down goods loop from Oxford North was extended right through to Wolvercote Junction, a distance of just over two miles. Also between June and August 1942, additional up and down goods loops were installed between Oxford and Kennington Junction. The major build-up of supplies for the D-Day landings in Europe saw Oxford reach an all time record for the movement of goods and military supplies, when during one week in April 1944 some 1,200 goods and military trains were recorded as having passed through the area.

On 10 July 1942 the Ministry of Works opened a meat cold store south of Oxford at Kennington, and on 5 May 1943 a 5,000 ton capacity grain silo was opened on the Bletchley branch adjacent to Oxford Banbury Road Junction at Kidlington. To serve the new stores additional new sidings were opened at each location. After the war the railway in Oxford remained pretty much intact, the only local closure being the Woodstock branch which closed to passengers and goods on 1 March 1954.

By the 1950s goods traffic at Oxford had increased to approximately 150 trains each weekday, with around 120 of these using the local yards, which between them dealt with up to 2,200 wagons daily. There were also regular freights each day running over the ex-LNWR branch between Swanbourne near Bletchley through to Hinksey. One tends to forget

Bowen-Cooke LNWR 0-8-0s were usually to be seen working freights between Swanbourne and Rewley Road yard. They also worked through to Hinksey. Here No. 49144 from Nuneaton is Hinksey bound as it passes slowly through Oxford on 3 April 1959 with a class K freight. (Author's Collection)

A panoramic view taken from the steps of the Station North Box in 1958. On the left is the steam depot (81F) and on the right the Jericho carriage sidings and at a lower level the ex-LNWR line to Bletchley. Passing through on a class H freight probably bound for Hinksey Yard is 2800 Class 2-8-0 No. 2855. (J. D. Edwards)

that parcels traffic also formed an important part of the operations at this time. In 1958 there were some 22 parcels trains being marshalled or re-marshalled at Oxford daily; figures show that during the year some 87,000 parcels were forwarded and 320,000 received, many of these being dealt with by the Goods department at Becket Street. From 1963 the parcel service was operated by the British Rail subsidiary 'Red Star Parcels'. Oxford had its own office which was situated adjacent to the up platform. In 1995 the parcels business was sold by British Rail to a management buyout. The privatisation of the railways resulted in the end of parcels being moved by rail, and in 1999 'Red Star' was sold to Lynx Express and then to UPS. Today the carriage of parcels on the railway is but a distant memory; the old Red Star office at Oxford was converted into a train crew depot and retail store until it was demolished in 2017 to make way for the new Chiltern Railway platforms at Oxford.

The 1960s brought a period of contraction with multiple closures, including the withdrawal of both passenger and goods traffic from the remaining local branch lines. It was also during this period that many of the wartime goods loops were either shortened or removed completely. Another casualty at this time was the ex-LNWR loop line between Yarnton Junction and Banbury Road Junction, opened in 1854; over the years it formed a major part of an important east-west cross-country goods route that avoided Oxford. During the period after the war it was being used by goods services between the yards at Swanbourne, Irthlingborough, Cambridge, Northampton, Rogerstone, Honeybourne, Cardiff, Severn Tunnel Junction and Pontypool Road, with locomotive changes taking place at Yarnton. During 1965 a decision was made to close the line; the last freight ran on 29 October 1965 and the loop, together with the exchange yard

An up class H freight from the Birmingham area to Hinksey passes Beckett Street Yard on 11 May 1963 hauled by ex-LMS Jubilee class 4-6-0 No. 45599 *Bechuanaland*. (Author's Collection)

BR Standard Class 4 No. 75001 enters the up yard at Hinksey in 1958. This large yard was opened in August 1942, with 'on the right' the 72 lever Hinksey South signal box. This was opened on 29 April 1942 and closed on 15 December 1973. Today, although some rationalisation has taken place, much of the old yard is still in use. (J. D. Edwards)

at Yarnton, was closed on 8 November 1965. The wartime grain and meat stores at Kidlington and Kennington were closed in 1967 and 1969 respectively. The need for large marshalling yards had gone and during 1967/8 the 1,000 wagon yard at Hinksey was closed to general goods traffic. Subsequent rationalisation of the yard saw the removal of the up yard, with the down yard being reduced to just seven sidings. In December 1973 the yard was remodelled once again with two through reception lines and six sidings.

In October 1977 the remaining sidings at Becket Street were closed, and the site is currently in use as the station car park. During the same year the ex-Great Western goods shed was closed, and during 1986 the south yard was reduced to just four sidings, one of which served an Esso petroleum depot. After being used for private storage the goods shed was demolished in 1985, and its site covered by a small industrial estate – such

is progress. In 2017 this was also closed and its buildings demolished, with the area now covered by University student accommodation. The remaining sidings at the south yard were removed during 2015 and the area now forms part of the proposed Oxford University Oxpens development.

Didcot power station was opened in 1968 and was supplied by coal via 'Merry Go Round' (MGR) trains from the East Midlands coalfields. By the 1980s there were up to 17 MGR coal trains passing though Oxford each day, with the equivalent number of return empties. In 1994 the decision to use imported coal from Avonmouth Docks to supply Didcot power station saw the end of MGR traffic passing through Oxford. Unfortunately, the decision to use imported coal hastened the demise of many of the East Midland pits. In March 2013 coal traffic from Avonmouth to Didcot also ceased when the coal-fired Didcot 'A'

BR class 9F 2-10-0 No. 92150 crosses from the ex-OW&WR (Cotswold) line, onto the main line at Wolvercot Junction on 16 June 1962 with the Bromford Bridge to Fawley oil empties. Wolvercot Junction signal box 'seen here on the left' opened in 1900; it contained a 54 lever frame, and was closed on 14 October 1973. (H. W. Burchall)

stopped generating electricity and was subsequently demolished.

Even with all of the closures Oxford is still a busy centre for freight traffic; almost all of the trains passing through the area now comprise container and car trains travelling to and from the docks at Southampton. These services are operated by DB Schenker and Freightliner using Class 66 and 70 locomotives. There are also a number of engineering and stone trains that run when required from the yards at Eastleigh and Westbury to Bescot and Mountsorrel. These are operated by Colas and GBRF using Class 66 and 70 locomotives. Hinksey remains open and is currently being used by Colas, DB and

Freightliner as an engineering yard and storage sidings. Currently there is also a service to and from the MOD depot at Bicester operated by GBRF, while the Banbury Road stone terminal, adjacent to Oxford Parkway, is supplied from Whatley Quarry and is currently operated by Freightliner, these latter services running when required. Oxford is often used as a diversionary route for freight, particularly when there are engineering possessions (closures) in the London area. It will be interesting to see what effect the opening of the East West rail link may have on freight traffic in the area; one assumes that it will result in more cross-country freight traffic passing through Oxford.

Modified Hall 4-6-0 No. 6959 *Peatling Hall* moves slowly through the station in May 1964 with an up class F freight from the Birmingham area to Hinksey Yard. (David Green)

Ex-Great Western 2800 Class 2-8-0 No. 2898 passes Aristotle Lane in May 1964 with a down class F freight service, probably to Banbury Yard. (A. E. Doyle)

Another shot taken at Wolvercot on 25 July 1964 of Castle Class 4-6-0 No. 7022 *Hereford Castle* on an up class F engineering train. (A. E. Doyle)

A Banbury to Hinksey Yard freight hauled by double chimney BR 9F 2-10-0 No. 92213 trundles through Oxford *en route* to Hinksey on 19 June 1965. The 9Fs were a feature of services to and from Oxford from their introduction in 1954 to the end of steam in 1965. (A. E. Doyle)

BR 9F 2-10-0 No. 92028 passes Kennington Junction in September 1965 with an up coal train. By this date both the up and down goods loops which were installed during 1940 were out of use. No. 92028 was built with a Franco-Crosti boiler in 1955; the Franco-Crosti apparatus was removed in 1960. (A. E. Doyle)

Hall Class 4-6-0 No. 6937 *Conyngham Hall* on an up class E express freight at Aristotle Lane in April 1965. The foot crossing leads to the nearby 'trap ground' allotments. No. 6937 was allocated to Oxford from August 1942 until February 1960, returning again at the end of steam in July 1965. The loop on the left was installed in March 1942, removed in 1976 and reinstalled and opened in July 2018. On the right is the ex-LNWR line to Bletchley. (A. E. Doyle)

A pair of BRCW (Class 33) Nos. D6544 and D6585 pass through Oxford with the Bromford Bridge to Fawley oil empties on 19 June 1965. (A. E. Doyle)

Class 40 No. D278 passes through Oxford with a mixed freight from the Midlands in September 1973. (A. E. Doyle)

Class 25 No. 25194 crosses from the up through line to the up relief at Oxford with a Railfreight service to Morris Cowley in May 1982. (A. E. Doyle)

Class 31 No. 31252 'with a Morris Cowley to Longbridge car train' has just left the branch and is pictured here south of Oxford at Redbridge in May 1982. (A. E. Doyle)

A pair of Class 20s 'Nos. 20177 and 20101' on the Theale–Lindsey oil empties in July 1985. What you cannot see is that the valve on the first oil tank was leaking and the train was subsequently diverted to the down loop and stopped for inspection. (Author)

Peak Class 45 No. 45065 approaches Oxford in September 1985 with some empty Cartic wagons *en route* to Washwood Heath Yard. (A. E. Doyle)

The Class 60s were once regular performers through Oxford on a variety of freights. Pictured here at Aristotle Lane crossing in May 2008 is No. 60074 *Teenage Spirit* in light blue 'Teenage Cancer Trust' livery. It is working the 6E48 Didcot PS–Linsey empty bogie tanks. (A. E. Doyle)

Class 58s operated the MGR coal trains to and from Didcot for many years. Pictured here at Radley in May 1989 is 58019 *Shirebrook Colliery* on a fully loaded Shirebrook to Didcot PS service. The locomotive is in Trainload Coal livery. (Author)

DCR-operated Class 56 No. 56301 passes Kidlington Stone Terminal in February 2013 with 6Z91 10.55am Calvert to Didcot PS empty fly ash train. The company had a contract to move the large amount of stored fly ash that was left after Didcot PS stopped using coal. The fly ash was taken to the old brickworks quarry at Calvert. Standing in the stone terminal is Class 59 No. 59203 on the return empties to Whatley Quarry. (A. E. Doyle)

Colas Class 70 locomotives await weekend engineering work at Hinksey on 6 July 2018. The railway at Oxford was closed for two weeks at this time for major track remodelling work. (Author)

Most freight services through Oxford today are hauled by Class 66 locomotives. Pictured here on 15 May 2018, Freightliner Class 66 No. 66415 passes Hinksey yard with a Southampton Western Docks to Birmingham Lawley Street service. (Author)

Class 66 No. 66538 approaches Oxford with a Garston FLT to Southampton MCT on 11 September 2018. On the left is the reinstated down loop, and on the right background Oxford North Junction. (Author)

GBRF Class 66 No. 66737 *Lesia* passes Walton Well with a service from Bicester MOD to Kineton on 11 September 2018. The service had earlier reversed at Hinksey. There are a number of freight paths through Oxford for the MOD services which run as and when required. (Author)

The Freightliner Class 70s currently operate a number of container services through Oxford. Passing through Oxford on 24 July 2014 is No. 70018 on the 05.46am Garston FLT to Southampton MCT. (Author)

DB Class 66 No. 66139 speeds through Radley on 15 January 2018 with the 09.43 Cowley MAT to Southampton Eastern Docks service, known locally as 'The Minis'. The train comprises 10 × 5 WIA wagon sets. (Author)

Chapter 8

PASSENGER SERVICES

The London Services

At the opening of the Oxford Railway
in 1844 the weekday service comprised
10 trains in each direction; of these, two
up and one down train carried third-class
passengers and goods. The Sunday service
comprised three trains in each direction,
while there was also an evening mail train.
The journey times from Grandpont Station
to Paddington were particularly slow,

taking on average two and a half hours for
the 63 mile journey.

Criticism of the slow running on the
Great Western at this time had been
mentioned in a Board of Trade report
of January 1845 during the discussions
for construction of the broad gauge
Oxford and Rugby Railway. The criticism
obviously worked as from 10 February
1845 all of the Great Western services were
speeded up, including those between

Beyer Peacock Class 2-2-2 No. 75 pictured here in original condition as built in April 1856. This locomotive
hauled the first standard gauge service, the 09.35am from Paddington to Birmingham, as far as Oxford on
1 October 1861. On arrival at Oxford No. 75 was replaced by No. 76 of the same class. (Author's Collection)

Great Western 'Queen 'class 2-2-2 No. 1127 stands at Oxford with a Wolverhampton to Paddington service in around 1895. These locomotives were used for a number of years on these services. Built in June 1875, No. 1127 was withdrawn in October 1904. (Author's Collection)

Oxford and London. The new timings now made it possible to reach Paddington in only 1hr and 15min, quite a change. These early services were operated using the very successful Firefly Class 2-2-2s.

The opening of the new station at Oxford in October 1852 saw the inauguration of a new service between Paddington and Birmingham. Comprising two through trains daily, stopping only at Oxford and Leamington Spa, they were timed to cover the 129 miles in just 2hr 45min. This gave a Paddington to Oxford time of 70 minutes with an average speed of 50mph over the 63½ mile route. These services initially ran via Didcot Station as the east avoiding curve was not opened until 22 December 1856. The next change came on 1 October

1861 with the introduction of standard gauge services between Paddington, Birmingham, Wolverhampton and Birkenhead, and also between Paddington and Worcester. The first standard gauge service to arrive at Oxford was the 9.35am to Birmingham, hauled by Beyer Peacock 2-2-2 No. 75 driven by Nicolas Graiff. Arrival at Oxford was five minutes late, where the locomotive was changed to No. 76 of the same class, now driven by Ralph Eliott. The train was further delayed at Leamington due to the removal of a carriage that had suffered a hot box (overheated wheel bearing). However after some fine running it was reported that the train arrived at Birmingham only three minutes late. The standard gauge service to Birmingham comprised three each day, running non-stop between Paddington and Oxford via the newly opened Didcot East curve. In 1862 the majority of these express services were being operated using the Class 157 2-2-2s built by Sharp, Stewart and Co. However, the broad gauge was not quite dead and lingered on with the up evening service from Birmingham still being operated using the broad gauge, with a journey time of 2hr 55min. This service continued until the removal of the broad gauge services north of Oxford on 1 November 1868. The end of the broad gauge at Oxford came with the withdrawal of all remaining broad gauge services south of the city on 26 November 1872.

Between 1880 and 1902 services between Paddington and Birmingham and beyond were accelerated and improved. No. 162 *Cobham*, a 2-2-2 built at Swindon in 1879, was recorded as covering the 129½ miles between Paddington and Birmingham with a load of 160 tons in 2hrs 12 minutes and 8 seconds at an average speed of 58.7mph.

Journey times were gradually reduced and by 1891 three additional services to and from Paddington, Oxford and Birmingham were introduced, all being timed to reach Birmingham in 2hrs 45min, very similar to the old broad gauge schedule. However, the 1898 timetable shows that the 9.30am, 11.25am and the 2.15pm down trains from Paddington to Birkenhead were timed to reach Oxford in just 68 minutes, with the heavier 1.40pm service to Worcester taking just 70 minutes.

The opening of the cut-off route in 1910 saw many of the Birmingham and Wolverhampton services diverted away from the Oxford route. This resulted in many of the fast services from Oxford to and from London now emanating from Hereford or Worcester. During the 1920s and 1930s the fastest train of the day was the 10.10am up fast; worked by a Worcester crew using a Star Class locomotive with a regular load of 10 coaches, it had a schedule of just 60 minutes. This service was discontinued

A service to Wolverhampton hauled by 4-4-0 Armstrong No. 14 *Charles Saunders* has a check over at Oxford in around 1910. (Author's Collection)

De Glehn Compound 4-4-2 No. 104 *Alliance* approaches the up platform with a fast service to Paddington on 5 April 1927. All three of the French locomotives were allocated to Oxford at this time for use on these services. No. 104 was at Oxford from July 1915 until its withdrawal in August 1928. (Great Western Trust)

during the Second World War, but after the war some of the fast services were reinstated, and by the 1950s the London services were back to the pre-war timings. The fastest service from Oxford to London at this time was the 3.07pm service from Worcester, the 5.35pm weekdays only service from Oxford, which had a 60 minute schedule for its non-stop run to the capital. Known locally as 'The Flyer', it was usually hauled by a Worcester based Castle Class 4-6-0 and was a popular turn with the loco crews. With a good run an early arrival at Paddington was almost guaranteed. Steam was withdrawn from this service on Friday 14 June 1963,

when double chimney Castle Class 4-6-0 No. 7018 *Drysllwyn Castle* made the run from Oxford to Paddington in well under the scheduled time. On the following Monday the service was hauled by Western Class diesel hydraulic No. D1005 *Western Venturer*.

In 1957 the Western Region named the 7.45am up and the 4.45pm down service from Hereford to Paddington 'The Cathedrals Express'. The 'Cathedrals', which was invariably hauled by a Worcester based Castle Class 4-6-0, was scheduled to cover the Paddington to Worcester section in just 2 hours 35 minutes, running non-stop to Oxford in 68 minutes. The up service, which also ran non-stop from Oxford, had a schedule of 70 minutes. In 1962 the up train was re-timed with an 8.00am departure from Hereford, with arrival at Oxford at 10.37am. The service now included a stop at Reading with the up journey time subsequently increased to 76 minutes. Interestingly the down service did not include a Reading stop; departing from Paddington at 5.15pm, 72 minutes were allowed for the non-stop run to Oxford. The name was dropped from the 1964 timetable after the introduction of diesel traction on the Paddington to Worcester services.

On 31 December 1965 steam was withdrawn from the Western Region and replaced by diesel traction, which resulted in most of the services to and from Oxford being speeded up. Another change came on 6 March 1967 with the closure of Birmingham Snow Hill to main line services. After this date all services from both the Bicester and Oxford routes were diverted to Birmingham New Street, running via the newly upgraded junction at Bordesley.

For the 1967 summer timetable one of the Western Region's 'Blue Pullman' sets was used on a new off-peak service to and from Oxford. Marketed as the 'Oxford Pullman' it departed from Paddington at 12.15 for its 60 minute run to Oxford, returning at 16.15. The service was basically aimed at the tourist trade but it was not successful and was withdrawn in 1969. During this period main line passenger services to and from Oxford were being operated using Warship, Western and Hymek diesel hydraulics. During the 1970s these were gradually replaced by Brush Class 47 and English Electric Class 50 locomotives. This resulted in many of the services being scheduled to reach the capital in just 53 minutes. In 1983 High Speed Trains were introduced onto some off-peak services from Oxford and in 1984 one HST service per day was running through to Great Malvern. Departing from Paddington at 10.10, it was marketed as the 'Cotswold and Malvern Express' and was timed to reach Great Malvern in 2hrs and 5min. The introduction of HSTs on the Oxford to

Departing from Oxford with a fast service to Paddington in March 1991 is No. 47701. It has had its nameplate and ScotRail logo removed, although the carriages are all in Network South East livery. (A. E. Doyle)

The new Class 800 IET trains now form all of the fast services to and from Oxford. On 11 September 2018 No. 800016 arrives with the 08.25am service from Worcester Foregate Street to Paddington. Standing in the down siding is Class 800 IET No. 800020. (Author)

Paddington services reduced journey times even further. In 1983 the 16.55pm non-stop service from Oxford to Paddington had a schedule of just 43 minutes. For the summer 1985 timetable and to celebrate the 150th anniversary of the Great Western Railway the 07.00 service from Hereford to Paddington, which at this time was hauled by a Class 47 locomotive, was once again named the 'Cathedrals Express'.

On 10 June 1986 the Western Region was abolished and replaced by Network South East (NSE), one of the newly formed business sectors. Apart from a change in livery NSE services to and from London were essentially unchanged. In February 1996 Network South East was taken over by Great Western Trains, a private company. Another change took place in December 1998 when Great Western Trains was purchased by First Group and rebranded First Great Western. Under the new company services were generally improved with more trains, particularly on the Cotswold line, which now saw the use of HSTs together with Class 165/166 units on most of the services to Worcester, Great Malvern and

Hereford. The rather unreliable Class 180 Adelante units also operated some of the services until their removal during 2017. The majority of these trains called at each station *en route*; now, however, the intermediate stations at Ascot-Under-Wychwood, Finstock and Combe are poorly served and at the time of writing there is just one morning and one evening service each weekday and none at weekends. Apart from the Worcester service the HSTs also operated most of the fast services to and from Oxford, with a schedule of 57 minutes including a Reading stop. In September 2015 First Great Western was rebranded as Great Western Railway. Today Oxford is busier than ever, with essentially a half hourly fast service to and from Paddington each weekday.

Up until the introduction of the new timetable on 15 December 2019, the fastest train of the day was the 'Cathedrals Express', the 06.42 am service from Hereford. Up until 28 August 2018 this service was operated exclusively using HSTs, but from that date the HSTs were gradually replaced by Hitachi Class 800 IETs. This service now departs from Oxford at 08.44am and including a stop at Reading is scheduled to arrive at Paddington at 09.37 am, a journey time of 53 minutes. However the new timetable has seen the introduction of a number of faster weekday services between Oxford and Paddington. The 06.48 am has a 50 minute schedule, and at the time of writing the fastest up service is the 07.53 which has a schedule of 47 minutes, both services include a stop at Reading. There are also four afternoon and evening down trains timetabled to run non-stop to Oxford in just 44 minutes.

Handborough on the Cotswold line. In recent years the car park has been substantially enlarged and with its close proximity to Witney and Woodstock the station has become very busy. In 2017/18 there were 232,000 journeys made from the single platform station. On 20 August 2018 an HST arrives with the 08.43 'Cathedrals Express' service to Oxford and Paddington. The long closed down platform can be seen on the left. (Author)

Pictured here passing through Radley at 90mph on 12 June 2019 is Great Western Railway IET Class 800 No. 802005. This high speed special ran non-stop from Oxford to Paddington to commemorate the 175th anniversary of the opening of the Didcot to Oxford Railway on 12 June 1844. The author was on the special that completed the 63½ mile journey in just 37 minutes and 35 seconds, a record time between Oxford and Paddington. (William Turner)

Stopping Services

Oxford to Didcot stopping services were a feature of the timetable right from the opening of the Oxford Railway, with all up trains calling at Abingdon Road. Appleford was served by three each day, which probably due to poor patronage closed in 1849. In 1850 services were extended northwards with the opening of the line to Banbury via Millstream Junction, with all trains stopping at the three intermediate stations: Woodstock Road (later Bletchington), Heyford and Aynho. A fourth station at Langford Lane (Kidlington) was opened in July 1855. The ensuing years saw the stopping service

extended, with further stations being opened at Kings Sutton on 6 August 1872, Somerton (Fritwell and Somerton) on 2 July 1906, and lastly Tackley Halt on 6 April 1931.

The opening of the Abingdon branch in June 1856 saw the construction of a wooden interchange station near Nuneham; this was only accessible by rail and was served by some Didcot to Oxford services. It was closed on 8 September 1873 when the Abingdon branch was extended northwards to a new station at Radley. On the same date Abingdon Road station was renamed Culham. By the start of the last century stopping services between Oxford and Reading

A rather dirty looking 5100 Class 2-6-2T No. 5152 from Banbury waits in the up centre road *en route* from Oxford to Morris Cowley from where it will work the afternoon workman's train from Morris Cowley through to Banbury. June 1960. (A. E. Doyle)

comprised what was essentially an hourly service. On 11 September 1933 the village of Appleford was again connected to the railway with the opening of a new halt. Not surprisingly, as the interchange station for the Abingdon branch, Radley had the best service with up to 18 trains a day in each direction, many of which connected with trains to Abingdon.

An interesting addition to local stopping services came on 1 February 1908 with the introduction of Great Western steam Railmotors in the Oxford area. The main service served communities south of Oxford and ran between Oxford, Thame and Princes Risborough, with Railmotor halts being opened at Abingdon Road, Hinksey, Iffley, Garsington Bridge and Horspath. Another halt was opened north of Oxford at Wolvercote, being served by an Oxford to Heyford, and very occasionally to Woodstock, service.

Local newspapers of the time indicate that the Railmotors were very popular and were well used. However, with the First World War in progress, on 22 March 1915 the steam Railmotor services were withdrawn from the Oxford area and were never reinstated. On the same date all of the Railmotor halts were closed with the exception of Wolvercote, which according to the records remained open until 1 January 1916.

For many years the Oxford to Banbury stopping service comprised five trains each weekday calling at all seven stations. One interesting service introduced during 1933 was essentially a workman's train from Banbury which took workers to and from the car factories at Morris Cowley. Departing from Banbury at 06.05 it stopped at all stations *en route* before arriving at Morris Cowley at 7.06am. The return working departed from Morris

A Paddington to Oxford semi-fast service comprising five coaches approaches Oxford hauled by Bulldog Class 4-4-0 No. 3446 *Goldfinch*. (Author's Collection)

Metro Class 2-4-0T No. 626 on station pilot duty at Oxford in around 1920. No. 626 was built in 1874 and was allocated to Oxford from November 1919 until March 1923. Coach No. 2902 was a Clerestory Brake Third built in 1895. (Author's Collection)

OXFORD TIMES, SATURDAY, FEBRUARY 1,

NEW RAIL MOTOR-CAR SERVICE.

To-morrow (Saturday) the Great Western Railway Company inaugurate the rail motor-car service that has long since been promised in the district. By this service considerable extensions will be made upon the existing passenger traffic between Shipton and Heyford on the north, and Princes Risborough, Thame and Wheatley on the south, while new districts will be opened up by the provision of "halts." These halts, which are stations in miniature, have been provided at Wolvercote, Hinksey (near the Waterworks), Abingdon-road (at the foot of Hinksey Hill), Iffley (between Kennington junction and Littlemore), Garsington Bridge (on the Cowley-Stadhampton-road), and Horspath village. For this service three rail motors and a "trailer" will be stationed at Oxford, and two will be continuously running. Two of these cars arrived at Oxford early in the present week, and a member of our staff was shown them by the courtesy of the station officials. The cars are substantially built, and appear to be of greater dimensions and power than those employed on the London and North Western Oxford-Bicester service. They are 74ft. long, and are divided into six compartments. At one end is the engine-room, rendered particularly spacious by the employment of a vertical type of boiler. Next to this is the luggage-van, and then the "smokers" compartment, with comfortable cane-upholstered seats, accommodating 22 persons. In the centre of the car is a small entrance vestibule, and next to this, remote from the engine, the principal compartment, similarly upholstered with longitudinally and latitudinally arranged seats, capable of comfortably accommodating 36 persons. At the far end of the car is the driver's cabin, permitting of dual control of driving and heating gear. The cars are lighted throughout by inverted incandescent gas burners, and are propelled by powerful machinery capable of maintaining a speed equivalent to that in the customary passenger service. It may be interesting, technically, to note that the driving

¾ inch to mile

machinery is equipped with an American reversing valve motion, and, unlike that employed on the L. and N.W.R., is visible from outside. The cars weigh approximately 45 tons.

The service is, of course, primarily intended as a feeder to the more popular main-line trains, but will incidentally open up new traffic between Oxford and several villages. The first car of the day leaves Oxford between seven and half-past, and reaches Wheatley before eight. This returns in time for the 9.5 express to Paddington. The second car leaves Oxford for Bletchingdon shortly after eight and also returns in time for the 9.5 express. The car from Wheatley then passes on to Shipton, and that from Bletchingdon returns to Bletchingdon. The trips are then varied in distance, and two journeys are made each way between Oxford and Princes Risborough, cars leaving Oxford shortly after one and half-past four. In order that Blenheim and Woodstock may benefit by the new service an additional trip will be run on the Woodstock branch to Kidlington early each evening. Parcels will be conveyed between stations as by ordinary service, but not to and from halts. We understand that the fare from Oxford to Wolvercote will be 2d., similar to that charged by the L. and N.W.R. The fares in the other direction were not officially announced at the time of writing, but we understand they will possibly be: Oxford-Hinksey, 1½d.; Oxford-Abingdon-road, 2d.; Oxford-Iffley, 2½d.; Oxford-Garsington-road, 4d.; Oxford-Horspath, 5d.

Oxford Times cutting dated Saturday 1 February 1908 announcing the new Railmotor service. New halts were installed north of Oxford at Wolvercot, to the south at Hinksey and Abingdon Road, and also on the Thame branch at Iffley, Garsington Bridge and Horspath. (Author's Collection)

Looking down from the road overbridge at the Wolvercot Platform in around 1911. Opened on 1 February 1908 as Wolvercot Halt for the newly introduced steam Railmotor services, it was renamed Wolvercot Platform in 1910 to avoid confusion with the nearby LNWR halt. It was officially closed on 1 January 1916 but had seen little use after the withdrawal of the railcar service. (Author's Collection)

Cowley at 5.10pm. With little change the Oxford to Banbury services continued until 2 November 1964 when under the Beeching cuts the intermediate stations at Kidlington, Bletchington, Fritwell and Somerton, and Aynho were closed. The remaining stations were served by seven trains in each direction, but with no Sunday service. Today the Didcot to Banbury stopping service is operated by GWR with the three remaining stations being served by up to 10 trains each weekday. Kings Sutton is also served by the Chiltern Railways Marylebone to Banbury service.

In January 1935 the Great Western introduced diesel railcars onto some of the local services, firstly on the branch to Princes Risborough. Earlier on 5 June 1933 two new halts were opened at Horspath and Towersey. The railcars operated up to three off-peak services daily over the branch until their withdrawal in 1957. They were also used on some off-peak stopping services between Oxford and Heyford and Oxford and Kingham.

By the 1950s there was an hourly stopping service each weekday serving all three intermediate stations between Oxford and Didcot. The seven intermediate stations between Oxford and Banbury had a service that comprised just five a day.

CHEAP MONTHLY RETURN TICKETS

ANY TRAIN—ANY DAY—ANYWHERE

CHEAP MONTHLY RETURN TICKETS are issued every day from and to any Station in England, Scotland and Wales (with few exceptions) at Fares of approximately One Penny per mile Third Class and 1½d. per mile First Class. Minimum Fares : 2/6 Third Class, 3/9 First Class. These Tickets are available either on the forward or return journey on any day within One Calendar Month and by any Train except Southern Railway " Liner " and " Continental Boat " Trains.

Break of Journey is permitted at any Intermediate Station in both directions for any period within the availability of One Calendar Month.

See Pages 2, 3 and 4 for Specimen Fares from

AYLESBURY		HIGH WYCOMBE
BASINGSTOKE	**OXFORD**	MAIDENHEAD
DIDCOT		NEWBURY
HENLEY-ON-THAMES		WITNEY

Cheap monthly return tickets, January 1939. (Author's Collection)

Great Western Star Class 4-6-0 No. 4066 *Malvern Abbey* is reflected in the drainage ditch at Wolvercote on its approach to Oxford with a service from Worcester in March 1932. This section of the line was raised above the Port Meadow flood plain. (Author's Collection)

Hall Class 4-6-0 No. 6930 *Aldersey Hall* departs from Oxford in June 1953 with the 08.55am service from Worcester, the 10.10am service from Oxford to Paddington. The Halls took over many of the fast and semi-fast services from the Saint Class 4-6-0s. (Author's Collection)

The Cathedrals Express was inaugurated in 1957 and ran between Hereford and Paddington. The up train left Hereford at 7.45am with the down service departing from Paddington at 4.45pm. Seen here is the down service hauled by Castle Class 4-6-0 No. 5037 *Monmouth Castle*, complete with a full rake of BR Mk 1 coaches in chocolate and cream. Standing on the down goods loop is 2-8-0 No. 3844. The loop was extended from Oxford in March 1942 but was removed in January 1964, although as part of the Oxford improvements it was reinstated in June 2018. (J. D. Edwards)

Photographed from the Beckett Street footbridge on 29 April 1958 is Worcester-allocated Castle Class 4-6-0 No. 7005 *Sir Edward Elgar* as it arrives with the 4.15pm service from Paddington to Hereford. On the left is the former Great Western goods shed and on the adjacent siding are wagons that have been loaded at Nuffield Exports Cowley containing boxes of CKN 'completely knocked down' Morris Cars for export. (J. D. Edwards)

Crowds pay tribute to a great man as Winston Churchill's funeral train from London Waterloo to Handborough passes through Oxford on 30 January 1965, hauled fittingly by Bulleid Pacific No. 34051 *Winston Churchill*. The coffin was carried in the second vehicle, an ex-Southern Railway van No. S2464S. (Author's Collection)

During 1958 DMUs were introduced on some Birmingham to Didcot semi-fast services, and from the start of the winter 1959 timetable, Class 117 DMUs were introduced on the Paddington, Didcot and Oxford services. The change from steam to diesel saw a reduction in journey times, particularly on local stopping services. For example in 1948 the steam hauled Oxford to Didcot stopping service had a 27 minute schedule, then the introduction of Class 117 DMUs reduced this to 20 minutes. During 1993 the Class 117 DMU units which had operated the Thames Valley suburban services for over 30 years were replaced by the new Class 165/166 turbo units. Today very few trains stop at all three stations between Oxford and Didcot and those that do have a schedule of 19 minutes. Most services now stop at either Culham or Radley, which reduces the journey time to just 15 minutes. Today, stopping services from Oxford to Banbury comprise 11 trains each weekday in each direction; however at the time of writing there are no Sunday stopping services. It is planned to introduce the Tri-Mode Class 769/9 units on services between Oxford and Reading by early 2021. In order to accommodate the new trains the platforms at Radley, Culham and Appleford have been lengthened.

The Castles were regular performers on services between Worcester and Paddington. Pictured here in May 1962 on an up Worcester service is Castle Class 4-6-0 No. 4082 *Windsor Castle* (previously No. 7013 *Bristol Castle*). The wooden sign on the bridge tells drivers to avoid dropping ashes or water onto the bridge. (A. E. Doyle)

By the early 1960s DMUs had taken over a number of local stopping services. Arriving at Aynho in 1961 is a Pressed Steel three-car Class 117 unit with a stopping service from Banbury. The station at Aynho was opened by the Oxford and Rugby railway on 2 September 1850, and a feature of the stations on the line were the cast lion heads on the station canopies. Today only the down building survives, as a private house. (C. G. Stuart)

Network Turbo Class 165 No. 165208 in Thames Trains livery waits to depart from Oxford with the 10.48am Thames Valley service to Paddington. Thames Trains operated the franchise from 13 October 1996 until 31 March 2004. (Author)

Class 165 No. 165133 'newly repainted but as yet un-branded' stands at the down platform at Oxford on 1 August 2018. As can be seen the station canopy badly needs a repaint. The Oxford to Didcot stopping services are currently operated using these two-car units. (Author)

Surviving from the opening of the Oxford Railway in 1844 is the station building at Culham. In September 1993 the original up platform was closed to passengers and a new up platform was opened. On 31 July 2018 Class 165 No. 165122 arrives with the 08.12 service to Didcot. In 2017/18 there were some 83,908 journeys recorded for Culham, most I would imagine to and from the nearby JET (Joint European Taurus) complex. (Author)

Class 165 turbo No. 165128 arrives at Appleford on 31 July 2018 with a stopping service from Oxford to Didcot. Opened as Appleford Halt in 1933, 'Halt' was dropped on 5 May 1969. It was rebuilt in 2008 when the old pagoda waiting rooms were replaced by the modern structures seen here. In 2017/2018 some 6,562 passenger journeys were recorded to and from Appleford. (Author)

Hymek D7061 on a down Worcester service at Aristotle Lane 'Oxford' on 19 May 1964. The Hymeks took over many of the Worcester services from the Castles after the latter were withdrawn from the route. (A. E. Doyle)

Class 47 No. D1728 with the 'Pines Express' service to Bournemouth comes off the Banbury line at Wolvercot Junction in 1964. Wolvercot Junction signal box and the 'Cotswold' line to Worcester can be seen on the left. The signal box was closed on 14 October 1973. (A. E. Doyle)

Hymek No. D7048 on a Hereford to Paddington service at Handborough for Blenheim on 15 March 1967. Handborough today comprises a single platform but is a busy station serving the Witney and Woodstock catchment areas. (C. G. Stuart)

The Class 50 Warship Class diesel electrics were introduced on services between Paddington and Oxford from 1977. No 50015 *Valiant* shunts its empty stock into the up carriage sidings after arriving from Paddington in August 1985. (A. E. Doyle)

Network South East took over the Oxford to Paddington services on 10 June 1986. To operate the services a number of ex-ScotRail Class 47s were allocated to Old Oak Common. Standing at Oxford in June 1986 after arriving with a Paddington service is No. 47704 *Dunedin*, still in ScotRail livery. (Author)

A pair of Class 31s, Nos. 31465 and 31434, arrive at Oxford with a service from Birmingham in June 1998. The train comprises a mixture of Virgin and InterCity coaching stock. (A. E. Doyle)

In full Inter City livery, an HST departs from Oxford in May 1988 with a service to Worcester and Hereford. The front power car is No. 43124 *BBC Points West*. (A. E. Doyle)

An HST service in full First Great Western livery approaches Oxford in July 2005 with a service from Hereford and Worcester. The rear power car is no 43026 City of Westminster. (A. E. Doyle)

Oxford sees regular steam specials throughout the year. A regular working is the 'Cathedrals Express' which operates between London Victoria and Worcester. It is pictured here departing from Oxford *en route* to Victoria on 1 April 2015, hauled by preserved ex-LNER Thompson B1 No. 61306. (Author)

Ex-Great Western Castle Class 4-6-0 5043 *Earl of Mount Edgcumbe* approaches Aristotle Lane, Oxford, on Saturday 1 May 2010 with a special from Solihull to Oxford and Didcot. The Castle with chocolate and cream stock brings back memories of the old 'Cathedrals Express' service. (A. E. Doyle)

Running without its usual headboard, ex-LMS Class 5 No. 45212 approaches Oxford on 15 May 2018 with the 'Cathedrals Express' service from London Victoria to Worcester. (Author)

Cross-Country Services

Over the years the Paddington, Worcester and to a lesser extent the Birmingham services have formed the backbone of passenger traffic at Oxford, but it is the long association with cross-country trains that transformed Oxford into an important railway hub. This started with mixing of the gauge south of Oxford through to Basingstoke on 22 December 1863, with access to the Basingstoke branch via a new loop line to the west of Reading and two new junctions at Oxford Road and Reading West. Although initially used for goods traffic between Basingstoke and Wolverhampton the new standard gauge connection soon allowed through coaches to operate from the north to Bournemouth and Portsmouth via the LSWR lines at Basingstoke.

On 1 May 1863 a new service had been inaugurated between Birkenhead, Dover and Hastings with through carriages being conveyed on the 08.45am service to Paddington. These were removed at Reading and transferred to the South Eastern Railway running via Redhill, and by the 1890s through coaches were being operated between Liverpool, Folkestone and Dover, via the South Eastern, and from Wolverhampton and Birmingham to Portsmouth and Bournemouth via the LSWR, all calling at Oxford.

In 1891, through trains rather than through coaches were inaugurated between Oxford and Basingstoke running via Reading west curve, and in 1897 between Oxford and Folkestone, again running via the South Eastern Railway at Reading. At this time services to and from Portsmouth and Bournemouth

In full Great Central livery, Robinson class C4 Atlantic 4-4-2 No. 264 stands at Oxford in around 1919 with the 7.45am through service from Bournemouth to Sheffield and York. (Author's Collection)

A regular LNER turn at Oxford was the Sundays-only 9.20am service from Sheffield to Swansea. Seen here after arriving at Oxford in around 1930 is LNER Ivatt Atlantic No. 3287; the locomotive was booked to work the train through to Swindon, returning on the 3.35pm service. (Author's Collection)

that were timetabled to call at Reading had to complete a rather inconvenient reversal in and out of the station; the problem was solved when on 1 July 1906 a new interchange station was opened at Reading West.

However the biggest change to cross-country services came with the opening of the Great Central/Great Western joint line from Culworth Junction to Banbury Junction on 1 June 1900. This new connection now allowed through trains to operate between the south, the Midlands, the north west and the north east. The new services were inaugurated on 13 August of the same year and comprised two trains daily non-stop in each direction between Leicester and Oxford. In 1902 these services which now also stopped at Banbury were extended through to Southampton, and during the same year another new service was inaugurated between Swindon and Leicester which included a through coach from Bristol. Also at this time

the 09.30am service from Birkenhead was split at Oxford into two portions, one to Paddington, and the other to Bournemouth.

The 1903 Great Central timetable shows four trains each way daily between Bournemouth and Sheffield via Oxford, with connections to York and Newcastle. Unfortunately the First World War resulted in many of the cross-country services being withdrawn. However, once hostilities ceased many were reinstated to something approaching the pre-war level. One of these was the Birkenhead to Bournemouth restaurant car service, which was reinstated for the 1919 timetable; it also had through coaches to and from Manchester. With the usual seasonal alterations these services continued basically unchanged up to the start of the Second World War. During this period many of the cross-country services were designated Furlough trains, primarily for military personnel and with limited accommodation for the general public.

Another shot of the 09.20am service hauled by LNER Sandringham Class 4-6-0 No. 2852 *Darlington* at Kennington south of Oxford in June 1944. (R. H. G. Simpson)

Southern Railway King Arthur Class 4-6-0 No. 30739 *King Leodegrance* waits at Oxford in May 1956 with the 15.08 service from Bradford to Poole. (Author's Collection)

One such service was introduced on 3 September 1940 and operated between Ashford (Kent) and Newcastle, departing from Ashford at 08.45am and calling at Oxford and Banbury *en route* before it arrived in Newcastle at 8.45pm. Prior to and during hostilities services from the north east were operated by LNER locomotives, with many running through to Oxford where an engine change took place. However, after the war locomotive changes started to be made at Banbury. The one exception was the Sunday 09.20am Sheffield to Swansea service that was hauled by an LNER locomotive as far as Swindon, the locomotive again being used on the afternoon return working. The service continued throughout the 1950s. I can well remember many a Sunday trip to Swindon Works during this period and being hauled back from Swindon by an ex-LNER B1 Class 4-6-0. Cross-country services to and from Bournemouth were generally hauled by ex-LSWR and later Southern Railway locomotives as far as

Oxford where a locomotive change took place. Northwards, ex-Great Western locomotives, usually Halls or Granges, were regular performers on cross-country services working through to Leicester or Nottingham. However, the *Railway Observer* reported that on 14 February 1937 two excursions from the south coast were hauled from Oxford through to Nottingham by Old Oak Castles Nos. 5006 *Tregenna Castle* and 5045 *Earl of Dudley*. It goes on to report that the turntable at Nottingham was too small to accommodate them so they proceeded light engine to Grantham for turning.

The 1948 winter timetable shows four weekday cross-country services calling at Oxford. The 7.20am Birkenhead to Deal and Sandwich and the 9.13am from Sandwich to Birkenhead, both ran via Reading and Birmingham Snow Hill and called at Oxford at 12.25pm and 2.20pm respectively. The north east was reached via the 9.20am service from Bournemouth West to York, which arrived at Oxford

Two rebuilt Bulleid Pacific locomotives pictured at Oxford on Saturday 8 August 1964. On the left Merchant Navy Class 4-6-2 no 35021 New Zealand line waits to back onto the southbound 'Pines Express' service that will shortly be arriving at platform 1. On the right West Country Class 4-6-2 no 34097 Holsworthy passes through with a Poole to Sheffield Saturday extra. (S. Creer)

British Railways Class 5 4-6-0 No. 73051 speeds past Hinksey South Box with the down 'Pines Express' service from Manchester to Bournemouth West in 1963. (M. Hale)

at 12.42pm, with the return working the 10.25am from York, arriving at 2.16pm.

The tradition of holidaymakers booking holidays from Saturday to Saturday resulted in a vast increase in summer Saturday cross-country traffic passing through or stopping at Oxford. During the 1950s there were numerous trains running between Birkenhead, Wolverhampton and Birmingham to the southern resorts of Bournemouth, Portsmouth, Paignton, Weymouth, Hastings and Margate. From the north east there were services from Newcastle and York to Bournemouth, and also from Sheffield to Portsmouth, Bournemouth, Cardiff and Swansea. Again many of these services required a locomotive change at Oxford.

From 9 September 1962 'The Pines Express', the 10am service from Manchester to Bournemouth West, which for many years had reached Bournemouth via the Somerset and Dorset line, was re-routed to run via Oxford. These services were still operated using steam traction, which required a change of locomotives at Oxford. However, after the closure of Oxford MPD to steam on 31 December 1966, locomotive changes took place at Banbury. Steam hauled cross-country services were finally withdrawn at the end of the summer timetable on 3 September 1966. The southbound Newcastle to Bournemouth service was hauled between Banbury and Bournemouth by Bulleid Pacific No. 34005 *Barnstaple* and the northbound service between Bournemouth and Banbury by No. 34034 *Honiton*. On 19 September 1966 the Banbury Junction to Culworth branch was closed and from that date cross-country services were diverted to run via Birmingham New Street over the newly upgraded freight line between Bordesley Junction and St Andrews Junction. On 4 October 1965 the 'Pines Express' service was extended to run

Unrebuilt Bulleid West Country Class 4-6-2 No. 34102 *Lapford* pulls away from Oxford in June 1960 with the cross-county service from York to Bournemouth. In the background are the gasworks and on the left the entrance and exit to the down yard at Hinksey. The gasworks were opened in 1818 and were greatly expanded over the years; they were closed in 1960 and finally demolished during 1968. (A. E. Doyle)

Looking down from the Becket Street footbridge on 31 July 1965, an unidentified BR Standard Class 5 4-6-0 departs with a service to the South Coast. Awaiting the arrival of the York to Bournemouth service where it will change locomotives is Bulleid Pacific No. 34040 *Crewkerne*. At this time Becket Street yard was being used as a scrapyard; the area today forms the main station car park. (A. E. Doyle)

Ex-SR Bullied Pacific No. 34034 *Honiton* hauls the last steam hauled down cross-country service from Bournemouth to York, seen here passing Wolvercote Siding, North of Oxford on 3 September 1966. After Oxford MPD closed to steam on 31 December 1965 the Southern locomotives ran through to Banbury. (A. E. Doyle)

Prior to the introduction of the Class 220/221 Voyager trains Virgin Trains operated the two-car Class 158 units on some of their cross-country services. Class 158 No. 158748 in Express livery approaches Oxford with a Liverpool to Portsmouth service in April 1999. (A. E. Doyle)

through to Poole but was withdrawn on 4 March 1967.

The withdrawal of steam and the introduction of diesel traction, particularly the Class 47 diesel electrics, resulted in a resurgence of cross-country services at Oxford, particularly on summer Saturdays. There were through trains from Oxford to the south running to Brighton, Weymouth, Poole, Bournemouth and Portsmouth Harbour; and northwards to Derby, Liverpool, Manchester, Leeds, York, Newcastle, Bradford, Hull and Glasgow. The longest run was the 07.34am service from Poole to Glasgow, arriving in Glasgow at 16.37pm, after a distance of 489 miles. In 1997 cross-country services through Oxford were taken over by Virgin Trains operating as 'Virgin CrossCountry'. These services were still being operated using Class 47s and coaching stock, but also Class 158 units, together with the occasional Virgin CrossCountry HST.

A complete change took place in 2000 with the introduction of the new Bombardier Class 220 Voyager and 221 Super Voyagers; these were gradually introduced onto all of the Virgin CrossCountry services. The Class 47s that had dominated the cross-country services for some 35 years passed into history.

In November 2007 Virgin relinquished the franchise to 'Cross Country Trains' who are owned by Arriva. Since then the services have been rationalised with destinations to Portsmouth Harbour, Brighton, Poole and Weymouth currently dropped from the timetable. The Cross Country services through Oxford now operate over two corridors, between Bournemouth and Manchester Piccadilly via Coventry and Birmingham International, and between Reading and Newcastle via the old Great Western main line to Bordesley Junction. Birmingham is particularly well served, with the service

Adelante Class 180 No. 180109 prepares to depart on a fast service to Paddington in April 2006. Standing in the down platform on a service to Newcastle is Virgin Voyager No. 220009 *Gatwick Voyager*. (A. E. Doyle)

The 10.12am Cross Country service from Reading to Newcastle departs from Oxford on 11 September 2018. In the foreground are the three upgraded down side sidings. (Author)

to and from Oxford comprising what is essentially a half hourly service, with an average journey time of 1hr 10 minutes. Apart from the few services that start and terminate at Guildford, all of the remaining cross-country services now reverse at Reading.

It is interesting to compare the following cross-country workings.

The 1956 summer timetable shows cross-country services arriving at or passing through Oxford on Saturday 25 August 1956 between 9.00am and 4.30pm. These were all steam hauled with a number requiring locomotive changes at Oxford. I have also indicated locomotive changes ('d/h' = double-headed, and 'c/e' = change engine):

Up Trains

09.30 Birmingham Snow Hill to Weymouth, No. 7915 *Mere Hall*

10.13 Birmingham SH to Portsmouth, No. 7918 *Rhose Wood Hall*

10.44 Birmingham SH to Portsmouth, No. 6979 *Helperly Hall*

10.54 Wolverhampton to Portsmouth, No. 4902 *Aldenham Hall*

11.04 Birmingham SH to Portsmouth, No. 6996 *Blackwell Hall*/No. 6853 *Morehampton Grange* d/h

11.20 Wolverhampton to Paignton, No. 6367

11.53 Birmingham to Ramsgate, No. 5370

12.15 Birmingham SH to Brighton, No. 5353

12.27 Birmingham SH to Margate, No. 6927 *Lilford Hall*

13.11 Wolverhampton to Weymouth, No. 6964 *Thornbridge Hall*/No. 6805 *Broughton Grange* d/h

13.47 Birmingham SH to Bournemouth, No. 6864 *Dymock Grange*, c/e No. 30783 *Sir Gillemere*

13.58 Birmingham SH to Bournemouth, No. 5981 *Frensham Hall*

15.08 Bradford to Poole, No. 61141, c/e No. 30738 *King Pellinore*

15.36 Newcastle to Bournemouth, No. 6980 *Llanrumney Hall*, c/e No. 30739 *King Leodegrance*

Down Trains

10.56 Bournemouth Central to Newcastle, No. 6324

11.33 Portsmouth to Birmingham, No. 7920 *Coney Hall* (non-stop)

11.54 Swindon to Sheffield, No. 5989 *Cransley Hall*

12.05 Portsmouth to Wolverhampton, No. 6937 *Conyngham Hall*, c/e No. 4990 *Clifton Hall*

12.25 Swansea to York/Newcastle, No. 7002 *Devizes Castle*

12.39 Margate to Birmingham SH, No. 5391 (non-stop)

12.50 Bournemouth to Wolverhampton, No. 30783 *Sir Gillemere*, c/e No. 5901 *Hazel Hall*

13.15 Bournemouth Central to Birkenhead, No. 30742 *Camelot*, c/e No. 1022 *County of Northampton*

13.26 Weymouth to Birmingham SH, No. 5912 *Queen's Hall*

13.39 Margate to Wolverhampton, No. 6390 (non-stop)

14.03 Poole to Bradford, No. 30738 *King Pellinore*, c/e no record

14.25 Weymouth to Wolverhampton, No. 6929 *Whorlton Hall*

15.05 Bournemouth Central to Birmingham SH, No. 30739 *King Leodegrance*, c/e, No. 1024 *County of Pembroke*

16.26 Portsmouth to Birmingham SH, No. 6853 *Morehampton Grange*

16.40 Hastings to Birmingham SH, No. 6866 *Morfa Grange*

Between 1979 and 1985 local railway enthusiast Jim Boudreau and others logged summer Saturday services either passing through or stopping at Oxford between 09.20 and 14.20. I have chosen 15 August 1981 as a typical example. Once again the list shows the order that they arrived at Oxford.

07.50 Leeds to Weymouth, No. 47152
09.20 Manchester to Poole, No. 47482
09.45 Crewe to Weymouth, No. 47315
07.55 Newcastle to Poole, No. 50046 *Ajax*

Up Trains

07.20 Liverpool to Poole, No. 47280
 (non-stop)
07.27 Manchester to Brighton, No. 47125
09.10 Birmingham NS to Weymouth,
 No. 47192
08.47 Wolverhampton to Portsmouth
 Harbour, No. 47140
08.16 Liverpool to Paddington,
 No. 50042 *Triumph*
08.31 Nottingham to Poole, No. 47254
07.10 Bradford to Weymouth, No. 47232

Down Trains

07.57 Weymouth to Bradford, No. 47228
08.42 Poole to Liverpool, No. 47296
09.20 Brighton to Manchester, No. 47552
09.42 Poole to Nottingham, No. 47146
09.09 Weymouth to Manchester, No. 47487
10.36 Portsmouth to Sheffield, No. 47445
09.58 Weymouth to Leeds, No. 47473
11.40 Poole to Newcastle, No. 47193

As can be seen the Brush Class 47 locomotives dominated these services.

Castle Class 4-6-0 no 5026 Criccieth Castle is pictured here being serviced alongside the coaling plant at Oxford in around 1957. It was allocated to Oxford from January 1951 until March 1958 when it was re-allocated to Wolverhampton Stafford Road. Standing on the right is Albert 'Bert' Bourton who was at this time Oxford's senior driver. (Great Western Trust)

Appendix

OXFORD LOCOMOTIVE ALLOCATIONS

GWR Shed Coding

From its opening Oxford was part of the Paddington Division. In broad gauge days engines are shown as working from Oxford. In the 1901 allocation book locomotives allocated at Oxford were coded OXF. This was initially placed in the cab but later on the front running plate. In 1932 Oxford was additionally given a numerical code, No. 111; this code was used for record purposes only. In February 1950 the newly formed British Railways re-coded all of its locomotive sheds, which were identified using the LMS practice of fitting a smokebox shed code plate. Oxford, which was still in the Paddington division, was given the code 81F.

Over the years Oxford had three sub-sheds, situated at Abingdon, Fairford and Woodstock. Woodstock closed on 17 June 1927, Abingdon on 20 March 1954, and Fairford on 18 June 1962.

Broad Gauge Locomotive Allocations

The Gooch Registers of Coke Consumption list details of where broad gauge locomotives were working at a particular date. The registers are divided up into fortnightly returns and provide an early allocation record for every broad gauge locomotive in service.

Oxford 18 February 1854

Passenger engines
Firefly Class 2-2-2 *Arrow*, *Electra*, *Hecate*, *Phlegethon*, *Pegasus*
Prince Class 2-2-2 *Queen*

Ballast Engines
Premier Class 0-6-0 *Ajax*
Hercules Class 0-6-0 *Hercules*

Total 8

28 April 1855

Passenger engines
Firefly Class 2-2-2 *Achilles*, *Dart*, *Hecate*, *Harpy*, *Hector*, *Tiger*
Sun Class 2-2-2 *Gazelle*

Ballast Engines
Premier Class 0-6-0 *Bellerophon*

Total 8

16 February 1856

Passenger engines
Firefly Class 2-2-2 *Achilles, Erebus, Harpy, Hector*
Waverley Class 4-4-0 *Pirate*
Prince Class 2-2-2 *Queen*
Iron Duke Class 4-2-2 *Balaclava, Perseus, Swallow*

Goods engines
Gooch Standard Goods 0-6-0 *Ceres, Iris*
Leo Class 2-4-0 *Dromedary*

Total 12

Abingdon, opened on 2 June 1856
Sharp Roberts 2-2-2 *Eagle*

26 September 1857

Passenger engines
Iron Duke Class 4-2-2 *Amazon, Eupatoria, Estafette, Inkerman, Perseus, Prometheus, Rover, Sebastopol, Warlock*

Goods engines
Leo Class 2-4-0 *Hecla*
Gooch Standard Goods 0-6-0 *Ariadne, Midas, Minerva, Nemesis, Vixen*

Total 15

Abingdon Branch
Leo Class 2-4-0 *Etna*
Sharp Roberts 2-2-2 *Eagle*

Total 2

10 April 1858

Passenger engines
Iron Duke Class 4-2-2 *Amazon, Eupatoria, Inkerman, Prometheus, Perseus, Rougemont, Swallow, Sebastopol*

Goods engines
Gooch Standard Goods 0-6-0 *Ariadne, Midas, Nemesis, Vixen*
Premier Class 0-6-0 *Argo, Vesuvius*
Pyracmon Class 0-6-0 *Pyracmon*
Leo Class 2-4-0 *Hecla*

Total 16

Abingdon Branch
Leo Class 2-4-0 *Etna*
Sharpe Roberts 2-2-2 *Eagle*

Total 2

April 1861

Passenger engines
Iron Duke Class 4-2-2 *Amazon, Crimea, Estaffete, Eupatoria, Perseus, Rover, Rougemont, Warlock*

Goods engines
Gooch Standard Goods Class 0-6-0 *Cambyses, Gyfeillon, Hebe, Janus, Monarch, Nemesis, Nimrod, Typhon*
Leo Class 2-4-0 *Hecla*
Priam Class 2-2-2 *Panther*

Total 18

Abingdon Branch
Sharpe Roberts 2-2-2 *Atlas*
Tayleurs 2-2-2 *Aelous*

Total 2

There is a large gap in the allocation records from 1861 through to 1900. I have selected the following years to illustrate the changing locomotive scene at Oxford.

Oxford January 1903

Dean 2-2-2 No. 10
Cobham Class 2-2-2 No. 159

Queen Class 2-2-2 No. 1132
3206 Class 2-4-0 Nos. 3208, 3209, 3211, 3212, 3213, 3214, 3215, 3217, 3219, 3221, 3222, 3224, 3225
Aberdare Class 2-6-0 Nos. 2635, 2639
388 Class 0-6-0 No. 710
2301 Dean Goods Class 0-6-0 Nos. 2319, 2325, 2337, 2351, 2357, 2374, 2499, 2500, 2532, 2535, 2563
2361 Class 0-6-0 No. 2374
517 Class 0-4-2T Nos. 549, 831, 1473
455 Metro Class 2-4-0T Nos. 455, 1499
378 Class 0-6-0 Nos. 477, 577
1076 Class 0-6-0PT Nos. 746, 756, 964, 1080, 1267, 1271, 1593
1661 Class 0-6-0PT Nos. 1670, 1690, 1691
1854 Class 0-6-0PT Nos. 1731, 1859, 1867
2721 Class 0-6-0PT No. 2795

Total 52

January 1920

De Glehn Compound 4-4-2 Nos. 102 *La France*, 103 *President*, 104 *Alliance*
517 Class 0-4-2T Nos. 203, 522, 835, 1438, 1473 *Fair Rosamund*
Metro Class 2-4-0T Nos. 623, 1450, 1491, 1494, 1497, 1498
Armstrong Class 388 0-6-0 Nos. 803, 1098
1016 Class 0-6-0PT No. 1044
1661 Class 0-6-0PT Nos. 1669, 1684
1813 Class 0-6-0PT No. 1827
Dean Goods 2301 Class 0-6-0 No. 2413
Aberdare Class 2-6-0 Nos. 2660
3100 Class 2-6-2T No. 3142
3206 Class 2-4-0 Nos. 3211, 3214
3232 Class 2-4-0 Nos. 3235, 3250
3300 Class 4-4-0 Nos. 3321 *Brasenose*, 3340 *Camel*, 3359 *Tregeagle*, 3369 *David Mac Iver*, 3370 *Sir John Llewelyn*, 3442 *Bullfinch*
City Class 4-4-0 Nos. 3700 *Durban*, 3702 *Halifax*
Badminton Class 4-4-0 Nos. 4102 *Blenheim*, 4108 *Hotspur*

Atbara Class 4-4-0 Nos. 4137 *Wolseley*, 4153 *Camellia*, 4166 *Polyanthus*

Total 40

January 1948

850 Class 0-6-0PT No. 1935
1501 Class 0-6-0PT Nos. 1531, 1742
2251 Class 0-6-0 No. 2249
2301 Class 0-6-0 No. 2579
2800 Class 2-8-0 Nos. 2827, 2861, 2881, 3835, 3836, 3838, 3847, 3848, 3866
3500 Class 2-4-0T Nos. 3585, 3588, 3589
4000 Star Class 4-6-0 Nos. 4004 *Morning Star*, 4021 *British Monarch*, 4049 *Princess Maud*, 4052 *Princess Beatrice*
4300 Class 2-6-0 Nos. 5323, 6300, 9316, 9317
4500 Class 2-6-2T No. 4511
4800 Class 0-4-2T Nos. 1448, 1450
4900 Hall Class 4-6-0 Nos. 4902 *Aldenham Hall*, 4903 *Astley Hall*, 4921 *Eaton Hall*, 4928 *Gatacre Hall*, 4938 *Liddington Hall*, 4973 *Sweeney Hall*, 5904 *Kelham Hall*, 5960 *Saint Edmund Hall*, 6925 *Hackness Hall*, 6933 *Birtles Hall*, 6937 *Conyngham Hall*
5600 Class 0-6-2T Nos. 5616, 6682
5700 Class 0-6-0PT Nos. 3608, 3687, 3722, 3741, 4645, 4676, 9611, 9654
6100 Class 2-6-2T Nos. 6103, 6122, 6138
7400 Class 0-6-0PT Nos. 7404, 7411, 7412
Ex-WD 2-8-0 No. 90529
Ex-GW Diesel Railcar Nos. W10, W11

Total 58

Oxford

January 1958
2251 Class 0-6-0 Nos. 2236, 2294
2800 Class 2-8-0 No. 3857
4073 Castle Class 4-6-0 Nos. 5012 *Berry Pomeroy Castle*, 5026 *Criccieth Castle*, 7008 *Swansea Castle*

4300 Class 2-6-0 Nos. 6336, 7324

4800 Class 0-4-2T Nos. 1420, 1425, 1437, 1442, 5808

4900 Hall Class 4-6-0 Nos. 4902 *Aldenham Hall*, 4903 *Astley Hall*, 4907 *Broughton Hall*, 4921 *Eaton Hall*, 4938 *Liddington Hall*, 4969 *Shrugborough Hall*, 5945 *Leckhampton Hall*, 5960 *Saint Edmund Hall*, 5965 *Woollas Hall*, 5966 *Ashford Hall*, 6920 *Barningham Hall*, 6922 *Burton Hall*, 6924 *Grantley Hall*, 6937 *Conygham Hall*

5100 Class 2-6-2T Nos. 4125, 4147, 4148, 5190

5700 Class 0-6-0PT Nos. 3608, 3722, 4676, 7760, 9611, 9640, 9653, 9654

6100 Class 2-6-2T Nos. 6106, 6111, 6112, 6138, 6163

6800 Grange Class 4-6-0 Nos. 6854 *Roundhill Grange*, 6864 *Dymock Grange*

6959 Modified Hall Class 4-6-0 Nos. 6970 *Whaddon Hall*, 7900 *St Peter's Hall*, 7911 *Lady Margaret Hall*

7200 Class 2-8-2T Nos. 7238, 7239

7400 Class 0-6-0PT Nos. 7404, 7411, 7412, 7436

9400 Class 0-6-0PT No. 8432

BR Standard Class 4 Nos. 75001, 75027, 75029

WD Class 2-8-0 Nos. 90251, 90284

Total 61

January 1963
1600 Class 0-6-0PT Nos. 1627, 1630

4073 Castle Class 4-6-0 Nos. 5025 *Chirk Castle*, 7008 *Swansea Castle*, 7035 *Ogmore Castle*

4800 Class 0-4-2T No. 1444

5700 Class 0-6-0PT Nos. 3653, 4649, 9653, 9654

4900 Hall Class 4-6-0 Nos. 4919 *Donnington Hall*, 4951 *Pendeford Hall*, 4979 *Wootton Hall*, 5922 *Caxton Hall*, 5923 *Colston Hall*, 5933 *Kingsway Hall*, 5945 *Leckhampton Hall*, 5955 *Garth Hall*, 5956 *Horsley Hall*, 5957 *Hutton Hall*, 6910 *Gossington Hall*, 6927 *Lilford Hall*

6100 Class 2-6-2T Nos. 6106, 6111, 6124, 6144, 6149, 6150, 6154, 6156

6959 Class Modified Hall 4-6-0 Nos. 6970 *Whaddon Hall*, 7900 *St Peter's Hall*, 7911 *Lady Margaret Hall*

7200 Class 2-8-2T No. 7212

7400 Class 0-6-0PT Nos. 7404, 7412

BR Standard Class 4 4-6-0 Nos. 75001, 75007, 75008, 75022

BR Standard Class 9F 2-10-0 Nos. 92220 *Evening Star*, 92224

Class 08 0-6-0 diesel shunter Nos. D3949, D3959, D3960, D3963, D3964, D3967, D3971, D3972

Total 50

This was the last year before the mass withdrawal of steam locomotives and before Oxford became a dumping ground for redundant locomotives.

INDEX